navigate beyond now

First published in 2021 – Self-published

All feedback about this book can be sent to admin@bespokechange.com.au

© Navigate Beyond Now by Maria Sievers 2021

The moral rights of the author have been asserted

All rights reserved. Except as permitted under the Australian Copyright Act 1968 (for example, fair dealing for the purposes of study, research, criticism or review), no part of this book may be reproduced, stored in a retrieval system, communicated or transmitted in any form or by any means without prior written permission.

All inquiries should be made to the author.
ISBN: 978-0-6452873-1-8
National Library of Australia Cataloguing-in-Publication entry: NLApp98178

Printed in Australia by Elect Printing
Text design by Maria Sievers
Cover design by Team Sievers
Interior design and layout Veronika Grebennikova
Editing by Tessa Wooldridge

Disclaimer

The material in this publication is of the nature of general comment only and does not represent professional advice. It is not intended to provide specific guidance for particular circumstances. It should not be relied on as the basis for any decision to take action or not take action on any matter it covers. Readers should obtain professional advice where appropriate before making any such decision. To the maximum extent permitted by law, the author and publisher disclaim all responsibility and liability to any person, arising directly or indirectly from any person taking or not taking action based on the information in this publication.

To my beautiful family

This book was hard to finish as I had to find the courage to share some of the deepest hurts we have faced together. In the end, I did it to help me to keep moving forward and continue my journey while hopefully helping others as they navigate their way through life.

We have experienced some unbelievable moments in our lives. Our incredible adventures would fill a book on their own. However, the most significant for me was finding my soulmate and the arrival of you boys. I always knew I wanted to be a mum, and when that day arrived, I felt my life was complete.

There is no greater joy than being a mother, and with the two of you, my job was relatively easy. Proudly I can say our family has the most incredible solid structure, and that is because we each contribute to its success.

Despite the monumental challenges life has delivered to our front door, we continue to find a way to push forward (I thought you'd like that, Jax). We're not searching for a pot of gold at the end of a rainbow; we already have all the gold we could spend within our hearts. We want to live our best lives.

Like all great teams, our family continues to stick together as we know how fragile life is, and we are determined to experience peace and happiness at any cost.

Together we know the clouds that roll in also clear away to make way for brighter days. There is nothing that we cannot achieve with the strength of each other.

Please continue to be the uniquely beautiful beings you are, as this is what your legacy will be.

Loving you for eternity xoxo

Table of Contents

7 Introduction

9 Part one: **My story**

    9   Adapt and flourish
    11   Something personal
    44   Work lessons
    54   It's your turn

55 Part two: **Your compass**

    62   Where are you NOW?
    80   Where are you headed?
    97   My identity
    116 Prepare for success
    155 Pack light
    162 Am I on track?
    180 Disruption, Change direction
    207 Keep going

227 Final thoughts

Acknowledgement of Country

'In the spirit of reconciliation I'd like to acknowledge the Traditional Custodians of country throughout Australia and their connections to land, sea and community. I'd like to pay my respect to their Elders past and present and extend that respect to all Aboriginal and Torres Strait Islander peoples today.'

Introduction

Welcome, and thank you for opening my book or rather your compass. Reading this book will connect us and make us part of the same tribe.

Who am I? I am my father's daughter and a proud descendant of the Wambaya people from the Northern Territory. The experiences of my ancestors have taught me a lot about how to overcome challenges and accept and respect all people and all places. My family is my most precious love, and there is nothing in this life I would not do to protect them.

As an influencer of change, my work allows me to do what I'm passionate about: advise and guide others while learning to become a better version of myself.

Navigate Beyond Now was born from my own life experiences and years of coaching individuals and organisations. My life involves helping people master change (both in the workplace or outside of it), become adaptive, and be ready to deal with whatever comes next. The information and guidance included in this book have been collated over many years from the knowledge I have gained, experiences I have lived, events I have witnessed, and from my clients.

It begins with my own unique story, including diverse examples, experiences, and challenges from my life's journey. Some challenges I could anticipate; others were utterly unpredictable. The story tells how I have learned to cope with grief, reassess my values, adapt, and flourish based on my choices and what is important to me.

In addition to my story, the second part of this book contains what I refer to as your compass. This section is for you to capture your journey using some of the great tools that I use myself and, in my work, coaching others. The stories and insights included here are relevant for anyone facing a challenging situation or has hit a roadblock in their life and needs something for inspiration.

My behaviours, values, and beliefs have altered over time based on life events, new information, or new reference points that have made me question their alignment or truth. It is perfectly normal for anyone to reach a time in their lives when they no longer believe their values or direction align with their reality. When this happens, it is an excellent time to 'check in' and reset your compass.

You will notice I refer to 'compass' throughout this book. We know that a compass is a device to indicate where you are now so that you can decide which direction you want to head. The purpose of the book is to provide you with some tools to gain clarity of your focus. It is a device for you to figure out where you are now and guide you in the direction you want to go. When thinking about the direction you are headed, remind yourself this is a signpost, a point in time showing you what you have set out to achieve.

Reaching your goal is cause for a grand celebration, and it is a time when others also acknowledge your effort. For example, competing in a race, or undertaking further studies, or reaching your fitness target. All incredible achievements to be celebrated. Although achieving the goal is awesome, the real change happens well before the finish line. It is the introduction of incremental changes that inform your ultimate result. Once I understood this and noticed the benefits of this approach on my clients, my outlook shifted, and I started to achieve more. To reach your destination, making small changes (I refer to these as one degree of change) is a great motivator, a catalyst for embracing new behaviours and creating new, positive, helpful habits. It is these behaviours and habits that stay with you beyond the achievement of any goal.

For me, committing to make small positive changes of practising inner peace through forgiveness and kindness enabled me to connect strongly with my life again. You, too, can find this inner peace. If you feel a little lost, overwhelmed, or simply require a reboot, use this book as your compass to get back on the right track.

Life is like a roller coaster ride at times, with sudden dips or a sharp change of direction to climbing what feels like an impossible hill before eventually catching your breath and feeling like, wow, I've made it.

Research suggests that writing (the old-fashioned way), may reduce stress and improve your mental well-being. As you have chosen this version, I'm sure you'll agree it is nice to touch paper.

Part one
My story

Adapt and flourish

My ancestors knew firsthand what it meant to be resilient and to adapt to survive. They were removed from their families and their land and forced to master new skills. My father, a single parent raising four daughters, learnt the art of adaption and grit. My descendants know this, too. Despite a tragic event that has altered his life forever, my son has also mastered the ability to adapt and to remain curious in this sometimes complex world.

> *Your circumstances do not define you; your attitude and ability to change will*

The catalyst for putting this book together was when my beliefs, values, and ideas contradicted how I was living my life. I was experiencing cognitive dissonance. Many factors led to the crossroads I eventually came to; life events, work, social expectations, and feeling like I was just existing and not living the life I wanted. Some factors in my life could not be altered, but what I choose to do about them can.

Something had to change, but where could I start? For me, it was apparent. My life's work is about advising and guiding others when they don't have a clear direction. I used the tools of my craft and started from there. I checked in to see where my life compass was pointed. Initially, I was like the mechanic who doesn't service their own car; change coaches are also guilty of not taking their own advice.

Once I got into the practice of checking in, it became a regular habit. I also use it to set my new year's resolutions. Think of it as taking an honest look in the mirror and making some choices about what you discover. It is not about running away from issues or pretending your habits are not affecting your life. It's about embracing what you find out and being kind to yourself as you formulate a plan forward. Once you have a plan, the critical step is to decide to act on it. Checking in on your life compass is simply a quick assessment of all the aspects of your life that are important to your overall wellbeing (e.g., health, family, connections, fun, work, finances, etc.). There is more information on assessing your compass further in the book.

Undertaking my check-in helped me discover elements in my life that negatively affected my well-being and prevented me from functioning at my best. There are times in our life when we cannot perform at our best. For instance, when we are grieving the loss of someone or something or when we are injured. Perhaps we have been diagnosed with a severe illness, are going through a separation or stress at work, or many other scenarios. When we are going through these times, we often struggle to see a way forward or remain hopeful of better days to come. From my own experiences, I can say there are better days to come, but when I was living through difficult times, I would not have believed this.

Below I have provided you with some details of critical events in my life that have significantly influenced the person I am today. These events come from my working life, upbringing, and some moving personal stories to help demonstrate how our experiences shape our thoughts and behaviours and can profoundly influence our direction in life.

Something personal

Unfortunately, or fortunately, depending on how you look at it, we cannot always anticipate what is coming next. Being prepared for change or uncertainty is extremely difficult. My family has experienced many life-changing events that are probably not dissimilar to some other families, but how we navigate each event may differ based on our circumstances, attitudes, and beliefs.

Growing up with my greatest hero — my dad, snapshots of mum

I will start at the beginning. I grew up in a loving family, and my dad was the best parent a child could wish for. He was our role model, teacher, nurse, caregiver, and so much more. He appeared stoic; however, I'm sure he mastered the art of hiding his vulnerabilities to protect us. He was practical in his approach to and outlook on life, and I know this rubbed off on me. He was at times the subject of local gossip, being a single father of four daughters in a small town, but that never seemed to affect him.

Those who knew him revered him

Whenever we spoke to anyone from our old neighbourhood, they always reminded us how special dad was and how much he could talk. His number plates were his initials, AH, but some translated this to **After Hours** saying he was always late because he was talking someone's ear off. He was a competent, clever, and witty man. He was a horticulturist, ran a wholesale nursery, raised his children, and still could do more. He was always there for us and others needing support. At times we had other teenage kids coming to live with us for short periods. Dad's business sponsored vulnerable kids needing some respite from their daily living situations. This act of kindness struck a chord with me, as years later, I became a weekend respite carer for vulnerable children. It was because of my dad that I wanted to become a mother so badly. Having him as our role model of parenting was the greatest gift ever. I understood how caring and capable a person could be.

I was the second youngest and can happily recall having a good relationship with all my siblings. For some reason, I assumed the role of mother (probably easy to understand why I later became the matriarch in my own family), my instinct was to parent. I'm sure at times; it was highly frustrating for my sisters. Strangely I was the only one interested in dolls, and they became the source of retribution if I overstepped the line with parenting instructions.

We were from a generation where families avoided acknowledgment or discussion about their indigenous past, as was the case for some members of my own paternal family. My grandmother on my mother's side was a Wambaya woman and part of the stolen generations. Sadly, we grew up without this knowledge as it wasn't a subject ever discussed. Even my dad, who was always respectful of other cultures, did not broach the subject of our past, and I'm not sure he knew enough about mum's family to share with us in his defence.

Growing up without our mother was challenging; however, she left when I was very young, so I probably wasn't as affected as my older sisters. Mum did pop in and out of our lives on occasion, and we all vied for her attention in those fleeting moments. She was on her path, which isn't my story to tell, only to say she was searching for something. It wasn't until many years later that I figured out what that was, to find and connect with the rest of her family. I, too, understood this need to find out more about our family. I always felt like a piece of my identity missing; initially, I thought it was because mum was not around growing up. However, as I got older, I knew it was more than that. I've always had a strong calling to learn more about my maternal family, who my ancestors were, and where I came from.

It had only been a couple of years when I was reunited with my mother before we lost her to breast cancer in 2001. Unfortunately, we never had the opportunity to fully close the gap in our past and reconnect to our true identities. I promised my mum before she died that I would keep searching for the missing pieces to our indigenous history. A few years ago, I eventually connected the dots, and at the time, I was elated by my discovery and apprehensive as this changed a lot for me. More about this later.

After suffering more than a decade of decline, in 2014 I lost my greatest hero, my dad, to Alzheimer's disease. Such a debilitating disease. In the early stages of the disease, I witnessed for the very first time my dad struggle. He knew he was losing control and could do absolutely nothing to stop it. They were subtle changes initially, like forgetting what day it was, then this grew. He was clever in the ways he tried to hide it, leaving himself notes around the house as reminders. I remember finding some, and reading them made me cry. One had my name and my date of birth with my kids' names on it. Realising I was losing my dad this way was unbearable; he was always my source whenever I needed wise counsel.

> *There was nothing a chat with my dad couldn't fix*

He had such a calming demeanour about him. It might seem strange to say, but I was relieved when his suffering had finally ended—knowing that he no longer had to live in what remained only a shell of his former self. I wanted to remember him as my vibrant, loving, ever wise dad.

A mother's first grief

When my husband and I were told that our son had a tumour and needed urgent medical attention, I started to hyperventilate and couldn't fully grasp what was being said. Everything suddenly became slow motion; doctors were speaking, but I couldn't hear them; I was watching my son play with his toy car in his hospital bed.

I finally turned around and saw the medical staff, and my only response was, you're mistaken; look at him. He isn't sick. We were in a small-town hospital, and I didn't trust that they knew what they said.

My son had complained about having a sore tummy earlier that day and then suddenly doubled over in pain, prompting us to take him to the local hospital. It was 3 January 1999, just before my son's third birthday, and I was eight and a half months pregnant.

> *I overheard the nurse say he had a tumour the size of a football*

Following the initial shock and prognosis, my husband and I found ourselves catapulted into a frenzy of uncertainty for the first time in our lives.

We were out of control. We lived 350kms from the nearest children's hospital, thus making it necessary for us to uproot immediately so we could begin our son's treatment. Our families were in Grafton, which meant we were going this alone. What choice did we have? My husband was the only one working at the time, so he had to quit his job to come with me.

Arriving at the children's hospital the next day was surreal; we didn't belong there; our little boy wasn't sick. He rode his bike the morning before and chased his dad around the house; someone had made a terrible mistake. We were about to celebrate the birth of our second child and enjoy those special moments of having a newborn around. The hospital was briefed of our arrival and was so incredibly caring and helpful. There was nothing we had to think about except to hold our son and listen to the endless number of specialists give us their opinions and detailed accounts of what needed to happen next.

In those days (at least in my experience), you only really heard about older people having cancer; you rarely heard about healthy kids getting it. Hearing the specialist talk about our son, the size of his tumour, and that they would need to start chemotherapy immediately to shrink the tumour before they could remove it was a living nightmare.

With no family close by, a very sick child, a baby on the way, no income to support us, and a property with a mortgage to manage, you could say we were in a world of hurt.

Denial is a powerful weapon to ward off pain. I should know; I spent the following 12 months in a state of haze and denial to survive.

Thinking back now and seeing what helped us get through that time, there were several things. The love we had for each other and our belief that we could conquer anything. The arrival of our second baby, who was our saviour and the lovely, caring staff in oncology. They treated us like we were family, they just knew what we needed, and nothing was ever too hard.

> *They were the true definition of compassion and empathy, and we owe them everything*

We introduced a simple story to explain what was happening to our son so he wouldn't be so afraid. The story was that he had swallowed an apple seed, and it had grown into a big apple, and he would have to take some magic potion to shrink the apple in his tummy so that an excellent doctor could carefully remove it. The only downside to that story is that he was always very wary of eating apples after that, especially if we hadn't removed the seeds.

Reality hits

Within weeks of arriving at the hospital, my son's tumour had ruptured, altering the prognosis to stage four. The Doctors advised it was vital to keep him as still as possible until they could remove his tumour. Easier said than done for an active three-year-old. We went through many frightening moments in the months that followed his diagnosis; being on chemo meant infections and transfusions were a constant recurrence. Living in a lodge adjacent to the hospital was not ideal with a new baby and a sick little boy, who didn't fully understand the fuss.

Four months after arriving at the hospital, our son's renal surgeon removed his tumour along with his right kidney. He spent an additional six months on a secondary course of chemotherapy post-surgery. Remembering my son struggling through his darkest days as a three-year-old little boy will haunt me forever. Some mornings I would go into his room, and he would say to me, **'mummy, today isn't a good day for me to wake up'**. What does a parent do with this? For me, these were the moments when I was most grateful to have our baby with us. Every time I sat him on the bed next to his brother, his brother would smile and find a way to get himself out of bed to play with his baby brother.

Once the chemo stopped, we thought that was it, life would return to normal, and everything would be ok. Navigating life after my son's cancer was difficult, and it was almost worse than stressing about cancer itself. That moment when they say your son is in remission. What does that mean anyway? For my husband and I, it meant thinking about the possibility of it returning every day for the next five years.

Admittedly I did not handle this time as well as my partner. The uncertainty and constant state of fear were overwhelming at times. Every time my son had a cold, a bruise, anything, I would panic. Fortunately, I could see what this state of panic was doing to my family, and I decided to seek help from a professional to look at ways of coping so we could move on with our lives.

I now see the support and learnings I gained from this experience and the changes I made back then as a fortunate stroke of fate, as they have stayed with me through many other life challenges. Some of the tools I was given to help me move forward with life are included in this book.

For the next 18 years, my son's life was primarily incident-free, despite the average kid's fractured arm and a relieved diagnosis of coeliac disease at age seven. Relieved because we had suspected it might have been so much worse. We were each living relatively everyday lives with the additional awareness that life was indeed fragile. We would seek adventure in everything we did, trying to live each day like it was a gift.

We were living life in the moment

Until that fateful day in January 2017, when I received a phone call that would again send our worlds spinning out of control. Nothing could have prepared us for this next journey despite our resilience and attitude to life.

More pain to come

In 2017, just two weeks before his 21st birthday, my son, who had survived cancer at age three, faced a devastating tragedy where he severed his spinal cord after breaking his neck. This would change our lives forever.

On reflection, I honestly can't tell you which was more painful. Seeing your three-year-old son lose his spark and innocence due to the gruelling treatment he underwent; watching the light dull from your own fathers' eyes as he loses his ability to remember his family; or discovering your son was paralysed and would never walk again.

The dreaded phone call

It was close to 9 pm on 9 January when my phone rang. The caller ID told me it was my son calling; it was odd for him to call me so late. When I answered and heard it was his friend on the other end of the phone, I immediately knew something was wrong. Have you ever had that feeling of dread wash over you so strongly that you feel instantly nauseous? That's what I was experiencing at that moment.

His friend started to speak, and although his voice was calm, I could tell he was holding back. He said that my son had hurt his neck after doing a backflip on a trampoline, but not to worry, he was ok, and paramedics were with him. Needing paramedics typically suggests you are anything but ok! His friend continued speaking, saying they were taking him to Canberra hospital.

I can't remember the call ending; all I remember was jumping in my car and heading to the hospital.

Arriving at the emergency department felt strange, the waiting area was scattered with patients, but it was like they weren't there. I approached the desk and asked if my son had arrived yet, explaining he was coming in by ambulance. As the woman checked for me, I overheard a couple of staff talking about a young man coming in who had suffered a severe spinal cord injury.

The woman checking for me returned to say he was due to arrive any moment now. I turned to look outside the window just as an ambulance approached. The first thing I noticed when the ambulance doors opened was my son's friend jumping out, holding my son's green Kathmandu backpack. Then the stretcher rolled out with my son on it, and in a flash, he was taken through the doors and gone from sight. I hurried to be let through to see him, and within moments I was standing beside him holding his hand.

He looked calm with no visible sign of anything wrong

He spoke to me but was a bit out of it. He apologised for worrying me and getting me out so late. I asked what happened, and he said he was doing a backflip and landed badly on his head. I wondered if he was in pain, and he said no, he couldn't feel anything. His monitor went off then, and doctors rushed in, and I was told to wait outside for a moment.

My son's friend and I sat inside a small cubicle inside the emergency ward, waiting to hear from someone. Eventually, a doctor arrived and said that my son had severed his spinal cord and is paralysed, and he needs to be operated on within the next 12 hours or may not survive. At that moment, I remembered the staff's conversation in the reception about the young man with a severe spinal injury, and I froze; that was my son they were talking about.

The doctor providing the update was extraordinarily blunt, and looking back, I can understand why. He needed to jolt everyone into action, and the time for comforting someone receiving terrible news was not at that moment. He explained that Canberra was not equipped to perform this surgery, and they would need to airlift my son to Sydney asap. Unfortunately, the aircraft had no room for me as they required multiple medical staff to accompany him. My son's friend offered to drive me to Sydney as I wasn't in the best state to drive.

Nine months in a state of fear

Our experience over the next nine months, mainly through the hospital system, was something I would never want another person to endure.

Even though it was the early hours of the morning, and I was out of my mind with worry, I can describe each detail of my arrival and first impressions of the hospital in Sydney. After walking around what seemed like the entire hospital block to locate the correct entrance, I finally spotted a reception sign and a person who looked as though they could assist me in finding my son. Unfortunately, my interaction with said 'help' was anything but helpful, leaving me more distraught than I was eight hours earlier when I first got the news of my son's accident. The reception said it was too early (this was a hospital, remember) to get information about my son's surgery; I would need to come back in a couple of hours. What I wanted to know was, had he already gone into theatre or was he waiting alone somewhere, how long would he be in theatre, you know the usual stuff a mother would be asking after. Sorry, we don't know; that was all I got. I then wandered around aimlessly, trying to stay calm. My husband had been away for work and was on a flight heading to the hospital, my other son was camping somewhere without phone reception, and my sister was due within a couple of hours. I was alone and afraid, and nobody could help me.

All that was running through my mind was what the emergency doctor had said to me at Canberra Hospital the night before: 'We need to act fast. Your son is in a critical condition and will need surgery within the next 12 hours if we have any hope of saving his life and, by the way, we can't help him here; he needs to go to Sydney.'

I returned to the reception area within two hours, and another person was on duty. I asked them the same questions as before. This time they made some calls and said, 'you've just missed him. He is on his way to the theatre now. Unbelievable!! I was too shocked to react.

I will leave you to think about what was probably going through my mind then. Suffice to say, I was not in a perfect place. At no point had anyone at the hospital asked if I was okay.

A simple act of kindness is all that was needed to calm the moment

After a further 11 gruelling hours of waiting, and after my husband had joined me, finally, we were told we could see our son. Walking into the ICU brought back many traumatic memories from a three-year-old little boy having his tumour removed. I was holding my husband's hand, and I remember looking ahead and seeing this bed with four doctors standing around it. As we moved closer, they parted, and there was our son. He had tubes running everywhere, his head was covered with bandages, he had a neck brace on, he had breathing tubes inserted, and his eyes were closed.

A doctor tried to explain the procedure he had just had. I thought he called it an ABCD; later, I was told it was an ACDF (an anterior cervical discectomy and fusion – an operation through the front and back of the neck to relieve pressure on the spinal cord and nerves, as well as to stabilise the spine). It included screws, plates, and a piece of his hip bone to ensure he was intact. He would be beeping at the airport with the amount of metal now inside of him. Despite the nightmare they had just described, my son looked so peaceful and calm. I remembered seeing him in Canberra late the night before, and he was quiet then, too. He said he was okay, but he could not feel anything.

I sat beside his bed and held his hand until he woke up, and when he did, a little piece of my soul died as I could see in his eyes that he now knew what had happened and that he was never going to walk again. My son is diagnosed as a C5 quadriplegic with an ASIA A rating, meaning he has a complete spinal cord injury. Unless medical science discovers a cure, he is likely to remain paralysed.

Due to the lengthy rehabilitation needed for individuals with this type of injury, I relocated to Sydney. I spent the next nine months (287 days) with him in the hospital to get him to a point where we could return home to Canberra. Let me clarify rehabilitation; this was to learn a whole new way of living with a spinal cord injury for my son and his family and friends. He was not going to come out fixed.

Regardless of all my previous exposures through my varied work and other significant life experiences, these nine months were where

I learned the most about human behaviour, including my own. These behaviours ranged from those with incredible empathy, others with total apathy and actively belligerent.

You will remember I mentioned earlier that I had adjusted my values and beliefs over time, and this experience was the single most significant influence in doing this.

Everything appeared broken

Naively I thought we would experience the same level of care and compassion we had in the Children's Hospital in Brisbane 18 years earlier when my son received chemotherapy. Sadly, this could not have been further from that experience. Not only were we struggling to come to terms with our son's severe paralysis and what that meant for his future, but we also needed to deal with intolerable behaviour and conditions from within the hospital regularly.

My son needed to be in a specialised unit for spinal cord injuries

Everything needed to be set up differently from a regular ward; although this ward had the essential elements, it was not purpose-built and therefore lacked in some instances. I was told it used to be a staff cafeteria before being converted. Most patients in the ward relied on the aid of others and equipment for many of their essential needs. Often this equipment either wasn't up to standard or was non-existent.

As I was the primary support for my son during his nine months of rehabilitation, I witnessed atrocious actions that I did not think were possible in the environment we were in. These unwelcome actions went well beyond the ward. At times, we were reduced to being treated like we were worth nothing or just part of a task list that needed to be completed. Check! I remember moments when my son needed to go for a scan, and a particular ward's person would turn up and insist he is moved to 'his' bed for transport, despite the ward bed being suitable for transporting. Remember, this is a spinal patient we are talking about; moving from bed to bed increases the risk of injury. A few times, they did drop and damage his limbs during these transfers.

Another extreme example included the wrong medications being administered via his IV line. Or the first couple of months using the wrong type of sling to hoist him out of bed and resulting in significant pain around his neck and shoulders and the inability to operate his wheelchair for several weeks.

He was in a constant state of fear for what might happen next

The most significant example was when my son was burnt by scolding water given to him in a flask by a staff member. As he didn't have any feeling below his shoulders, and the flask was sitting in his lap, he didn't realise he was burnt until it was too late. He had suffered third-degree burns.

Even basic patient security was at times lacking with the ward sharing space with injured prison inmates. At times these patients were aggressive with staff, and more than once, we were harassed by these individuals who were often given privileges like smoking on the ward whilst it appeared the team had turned a blind eye. It's worth mentioning that when you suffer a spinal cord injury at the level my son had, your diaphragm is affected, making it difficult to breathe or cough, so having smokers around you was not a good idea. These were significant examples of complacency and poor attitudes ingrained into some of the minds of those working within the hospital.

When compassion is missing

Mostly you could overlook when a mistake is made, as this happens in any environment; however, it was the moments when my son was treated without compassion or empathy that hurt the most. Every morning I would take a deep breath before entering the ward, hoping nothing had gone awry overnight. Each time my son suffered, I suffered alongside him. I watched him screaming out in pain, and not being able to do anything does something to you. It leaves you feeling empty and powerless. You don't feel it's possible to come back from this sort of hurt. When he came across those that couldn't provide comfort or see his pain, that was where the actual damage was being done.

Do not get me wrong; some exceptional nurses and doctors cared for him daily and the surgeons we owe our son's survival. Watching these dedicated people work tirelessly would bring tears to my eyes and melt my heart; it still does. These individuals restored my faith in humanity.

It was those who lacked compassion who left a terrible scar on my son and me. It took me a long time (and even longer therapy) to realise that some of the staff within the hospital had lost their way in understanding what their role was anymore.

Sadly, for them, their role had become purely transactional

They had somehow forgotten that patients were people with feelings, and this patient (my son) had just lost his entire identity and was struggling to survive. It appeared that my son's comfort or needs no longer played a part in their world; they were indifferent. At first, I was angry and lashed out at anyone who would listen; over time, I took pity on them. I realised nothing could be worse than losing compassion or empathy for others.

I remember watching a documentary on this issue in aged care facilities and seeing the effects of an individual providing long-term care to the same patient. For some, this didn't impact their effectiveness or compassion; for others, it was a very different story.

The culture of a workplace also plays a big part in this. Thankfully I can say when my father was being cared for in his nursing home, they were all incredibly caring. As a change manager and coach, I understood what poor organisational culture could do to a person. They become indifferent and feel like it doesn't matter what they do and think they can't make a difference, so they don't bother. Or they bully their way through and take their frustrations out on others.

I don't believe people go to work intending to do a lousy job; they lose their way and assimilate into their environment. This type of culture is generally driven by pressures from the top and filters into all pockets of an organisation, resulting in a toxic culture and a fractured system. I expand more on this in my **work lessons**.

These were broken people working in a place that needed support from other broken people and a broken system. A tragedy. It must have been highly frustrating to those trying to do a good job, as they had to work alongside those who no longer seemed to care. I made several attempts to try and improve the situation; however, often, these efforts were futile. From my observations, the whole system needed an overhaul.

I constantly found myself in a position where I tried to convince people to do better, care more, and change their attitudes. In the end, I could see how much this was affecting my son and me on a deeper level.

> *I was losing control and could not see a way out of this dark place*

My family, friends, and work colleagues would describe me as a happy-go-lucky person, always ready with a smile and willing to offer support and empathy for those around me. However, this experience was changing me, I was starting to lose my sh#t, and I was becoming a person I didn't like. My smiles became forced, and at times I wanted payback to all those hurting my son.

I would talk to other families or patients, and although they would say they were also experiencing the same sort of problems, they did not want to rock the boat. They feared the consequences of speaking up.

The challenges we faced during those nine months often hurt, sometimes harmed, and felt endless.

Although not speaking up goes entirely against everything I believe in, at the time, I felt I was alone on this mission.

Please someone help us

I used my diary to document each day's events. I wrote what hurt, what helped, and what I was grateful for. I also wrote my encouraging sayings (some are in this book). I would colour in, do deep breathing, go for walks, and set small goals each day. All of these were my attempt to carry on amid chaos.

We soon discovered more complexity around having a spinal cord injury. A saying that veteran SCI's (spinal cord injuries) would use, 'one wheel forward, three wheels back'. This was true for my son. Six weeks after his initial surgery, he needed another surgery due to some infected hardware (screws and plates) at his injury site.

Regrettably, a few days after this surgery, a tear was discovered in his oesophagus that allowed air and fluid into his spinal cavity. This was not a good place to have a hole. The weeks following this were the darkest of all. My son was nil by mouth, not even allowed to swallow his spit. He would become so anxious when he saw someone eating or drinking in front of him that it required constant support from his family to keep him from having a panic attack. I would spend an average of 14 hours a day with him to keep him calm. I would read to him, hold his hand, practice reiki; I even had a Buddhist therapist sit with him, anything to soothe him. In addition to the tear, he was trying to cope with, his body was also figuring out its temperature.

Yet another bizarre discovery for spinal cord injuries is that your temperature gauge goes haywire. It could be 36 degrees outside, and they could be freezing. My son would wear a beanie and a blanket in the middle of summer. By this stage, he had lost a lot of weight. He went into hospital weighing 77kg; within weeks, he weighed only 60kg. Not good, considering he was six foot two tall.

The medical team was hoping that over time the tear would heal itself. Regrettably, it didn't, and my son's health radically deteriorated. In the end, they decided to operate again to fix the tear. This happened on the 1st of April, three months after his initial surgery.

My husband and I knew that we were losing our son, and this surgery was his only chance. It was not exactly the best odds, and there were some experimental aspects to it. I cannot remember how many waivers we signed for each of the different surgical teams needed for this intervention, but there was no other choice. Once we saw our son go through the theatre room doors, my husband and I drove to the beach to sit and wait. We were told it would be about ten hours.

It's interesting how your mind can block everything out whilst you are in the midst of chaos, and yet as soon as you step outside for a moment, a tsunami hits, and everything comes flooding back in. Sitting on the edge of the sand, my husband and I were both distraught with anguish. It didn't help that we had spent little time together since that dreaded day of the accident. We felt like strangers sitting together in silence and sadness. As the minutes ticked by, I knew I needed to do something to pass the time, so I decided to write the spinal team a message. I wrote it through my son's eyes as I wanted them to know what he was experiencing in their care. This is what it said:

Please help me, this is my first time here, and I'm scared.

While I lie here and try to understand what has happened, I can hear strange noises – buzzers, trolleys rolling, beeping, medical staff talking.

I constantly wonder if this is real, and then I remember that it is my buzzer and my machine that is beeping.

A stranger approaches my bed, stands next to the machine, press some buttons, and then walks away. I try to get their attention, but my head doesn't move, and my arm is weak, and I don't seem to be able to raise it. Is it also paralysed?

I need my mask adjusted and some ice to suck as my throat is dry from this machine pushing air into my lungs. I'm afraid I'll choke, and I can't call for help. My body is lifeless, so I have no way of getting attention.

Eventually, someone returns and adjusts the mask. I ask if the blankets can be pulled up as I am freezing, and I am told to 'wait a minute, I will get to it when I finish this.'

I feel sad because I do not understand why this person is gruff with me and cannot see my pain and the fear in my eyes from trying to understand why I am here and why I can't feel most of my body.

It is times like these that I need my mum and dad the most. How did it come to this? Why do I feel like a helpless child? A couple of weeks ago, I was living *with my flatmates, enjoying life and holidaying with my girlfriend through Turkey. Now I lie here wanting my parents at my side to comfort and soothe my pain.*

I manage to get through the night and find sunshine when I wake; an amazing nurse heads my way; he talks to me to reassure me and explain what he is doing and what will happen next. This soothes me and helps me to stay calm.

In addition to the wonderful nurses and dressers, other notable people come and go throughout the day, including the incredible physio team, therapist, dietician, speech therapist, OT, social worker, registrar, etc., and spinal consultants.

Every day for the past three months has been beyond difficult for me, and generally, the people around me make all the difference in keeping me positive and fighting to stay strong.

However, now and then, some step into the picture and don't always recognise my pain and suffering, and to them, I'd like to say.... please help me; this is my first time here, and I'm scared.

I gave this message to my son's social worker, and she shared it with the entire spinal ward. She also gave the message to the nursing unit and other members of the hospital team.

Delivering the message this way seemed to have struck a chord with a few individuals who had forgotten the meaning of care; others acknowledged our plea for help.

Fortunately, the surgery was a success and, when my son woke up, we committed together to push forward and endure the next five months so we could return to our home and try to figure out our new lives.

Find your voice, speak up

Incredibly, even after our plea for help, my son continued to experience poor behaviour within the hospital. It took multiple complaints and constant pushing from me to get any action. As for taking accountability, well, let's say that was a foreign concept. Those that could do something went above and beyond to advocate for us; they were incredible, they made all the difference to my sanity, but I'm sure it came at a price to them also. Often, the frequent incidents were dismissed as unfortunate or, better still, it was the responsibility of another area. Whenever I broached the subject with hospital administration, they made me feel like I was obstructive. It wasn't until after we left the hospital that we were invited to have our say at a complaint resolution meeting, the outcome being an apology and more staff training. I suppose that was something. Having spent most of my working life in roles that focused on improving organisational culture and leadership alignment, I was very familiar with environments where accountability was absent, and this resembled one of them.

As we endured the remainder of our hospital stay, I continued to have a voice, and when I needed to speak up, I did. My mission was to ensure my son got the care he needed, and nothing was going to get in the way of that.

> *Being brave takes courage, but we need to do it more often if we want things to change. See something, say something*

The combined cumulative effect of what was happening at the hospital and trying to reconcile a new way of living had an incredible impact on how we functioned daily. We were grieving and barely holding it together, but I was determined not to let this beat us.

I had committed to my son to stay strong to get through the nightmare, but I could feel the internal build-up of turmoil.

More grief

Grief is a bizarre thing. People around you can tell you that everything will be ok; it's normal to feel this way. Or things can't be that bad; it's only because you're grieving that you think this way. Everyone wants to solve your grief.

For me, I stopped listening to anyone telling me how I should or should not be feeling, as it did not add any value. Instead, I started to read books on grief. Although most were about losing a loved one, so it wasn't easy to relate fully. Except for one book, **It's ok that you're not ok** by **Megan Devine**, this was extremely helpful for me. For the first time, I didn't feel like I was going crazy.

Three weeks after my son's third surgery, we received news that our dearest friends were coming to visit us from Dubai. They arrived on 21st April, it was a Friday night, and after visiting hours at the hospital, my husband and I caught up with them for dinner. We talked about old times with our families, we laughed, and we updated them on what was happening with both our sons. By the time we parted for the night, they felt a little anxious about visiting our son in the hospital the next day.

At 6 am the following morning, we got a call from our friends to say their son had been in a car accident back in Dubai and they needed to leave immediately. We were utterly shocked and now feeling very anxious for them to return home as soon as possible to be there for their son.

Tragically, after many weeks in a coma, our friends had lost their only child. It just didn't seem possible that our beautiful friends were coming to comfort us in our need and then ended up losing their son. At times I question how the universe works.

Early in June, our friends flew back to Sydney with their son so family and friends could attend his funeral and say their goodbyes.

We assumed our son would not be ready to attend the funeral as he was still recovering from his last surgery; however, he insisted on being there for our friends. This would be his first time out of hospital since the injury.

I hadn't anticipated the logistics involved just getting to the church and being out in the community together as a family. My husband and I went to the church a few days beforehand to ensure our son's wheelchair would fit; it turned out we needed to use a different entrance, so we were thankful we sorted it out before the day. My youngest son flew up from Melbourne, and we all attended the funeral together. It was an overwhelming experience in so many ways.

> *To see our friends suffering on a level I could not understand, broke my heart*

Sitting next to my son in the church, I could feel myself breaking; I looked at our friends comforting each other and saw how they were trembling with grief. It was at this moment that I indeed saw my pain.

I looked at the coffin and back at my friends, and over to my son, and it was too much. The loss around us consumed me, and I told myself to hold on a little longer; this wasn't the day to break; I needed to remain strong for our friends.

Grief can be so consuming you begin to lose touch with the world around you.

Attempting to mask the pain

Thinking about our friend's grief and seeing my son's loss and the suffering he was enduring every day became unbearable. I needed something urgently to help me to maintain some semblance of control. In the end, I decided to return to work to help distract me from the constant chaos. I began working casual hours on a delicate project to support veterans and their families transitioning from the Australian Defence Force to civilian life. I was very interested in this project, focusing on improving veterans' well-being and reducing veteran suicides. Helping others is my life's work and something I remain passionate about, so I was looking forward to this positive distraction.

While I was working, more cracks started to appear, although nobody knew, apart from a few close friends on the surface. Even they only saw the parts I was willing to share. Nobody would believe you anyway, or they would think I was exaggerating the truth; that much drama happening simultaneously wasn't typical. I found myself crying at the drop of a hat, consumed with the feeling of hopelessness, anger, and completely numb.

> *I was drowning in grief*

I remember a reoccurring nightmare I was having at the time. In the hell, I found myself trapped inside a water tank, and there was only a small air space between the water and the top of the tank.

I would wake up from this in a state of panic and would immediately need to open a window and take in deep gulps of air. The effects of those nightmares linger today, as I can't sleep without a window open, and wearing a mask is a struggle.

Stupidly or courageously (I'll leave that for you to decide), I put one foot in front of the other and carried on. I tried to avoid anyone who appeared happy as I did not want to be reminded of what we were missing out on. I went about my day with a determined smile and maintained the ability to offer comfort and support to others, however at night, when I was often alone, I would cry myself to sleep and wish our nightmare would soon end.

There were a few occasions when I did lose my composure in public. One was when I lashed out at a woman who asked me to move off a path I was stretching on, she was abrasive, and I reacted to this in an aggressive tone that later shocked me. Another was trying to deal with Centrelink on behalf of my son, waiting in line to be served; I felt myself becoming more and more agitated. It was like I was being punished, and when I finally got to the counter, and the person said there was one page missing, I broke down and walked out. Between that, dealing with NDIS, the hospital, finding accessible housing, working, caring for my son, and being there for the rest of my family, I struggled to keep it together.

I remember another time at work when I was organising a project team event. I was working with a retired general at the time. He had a particular way with a crowd; some would say he was reasonably intimidating; however, he had an important message to share. After working with veterans and understanding what they go through, I understood this. In the end, my manager and I sat down and discussed how some of the team perceived him. We asked if we could run a session where we all got to know each other better so the team could see he was a very empathetic person. The session was going well, and then the retired general asked everyone about their plans for the coming Christmas break. It wasn't until that moment that I had even thought about Christmas and what that now looked like for our family. We would often take a trip together to explore a new city or culture during Christmas, but that was not going to be possible this time; I wasn't sure we'd ever get to do that together again.

As we were going around the room and each team member provided details of how they would spend Christmas, I started to feel uneasy. My lip quivered, and I wasn't sure I could do this. It was suddenly my turn to speak, and I started on a positive note about how much Christmas means to my family and me, and then I just burst into tears and rushed out of the room.

> *I was breaking inside, and I wasn't ready to face the next step in our journey*

More and more, I was shutting down. I was becoming angry and disengaged with most things in life. I knew I was falling apart and wasn't sure how long I could keep this up.

A moment of joy

One morning I walked to the beach, as I did most days when I was at the hospital, and I saw the most beautiful flower blooming in someone's garden. I can't tell you what sort of flower it was, but it was a brilliant pink and perfect. It immediately reminded me of a time after I lost my dad when I was working in Sydney, and I walked past a garden then and could smell the most incredible fragrant rose. It was weird as it wasn't the time of year roses usually bloomed. Seeing this flower sparked something in me. It was so small I hardly recognised it at first, but **I felt joy**. I stood looking at this flower for a few moments more before my mind took back control and reminded me of the day's tasks ahead.

> *When your senses open through the fog and you see colour again, it is pure bliss*

The sad part was as soon as I realised that I had blocked out my worries for a moment, I became overwhelmed with guilt; how could I allow myself to feel joy at this moment.

Reaching a tipping point

As the days and weeks dragged on, I knew that this cycle had to stop. This new pattern of behaviour was a nasty habit that would ruin my life if I didn't find a way to change direction. Even though I don't think he realised it, my younger son had the most influence over my wake-up call. When you shut down, you inadvertently also shut out the people around you. I had mastered the art of avoidance and closing off everything beyond the immediate chaos in front of me.

I've always been a journal writer. One night when I was writing in my journal, I was doing a visualization exercise (where you see yourself in a particular situation, i.e., in the future doing something and how you respond, the outcome, etc.). On this occasion, I thought about my sons being married and having families of their own, and my husband and I were visiting them. This scared me as I realised at that moment that I had pushed any future dreams aside, believing they were impossible, my son couldn't have children, so I stopped believing. I had blocked out any hopes or plans of the future based on where we were right then, and this had to change, as firstly I was reminded, I had two sons, and secondly, **there is no such thing as can't** (words of wisdom from my dad). In addition to wanting to be a mum, I also wanted to experience being a grandmother, and somewhere along the journey, I stopped allowing myself to believe this could happen.

Of course, this was one of my dreams and not necessarily one shared by my sons, but the point was it startled me into action. I had a future; we all had a lot to look forward to.

It was then that I knew what I needed to do to keep going. Firstly, I had to engage some professional help, and this was a little confronting as I felt weak for needing help again. I wasn't the one injured; my son was. So why did I feel so out of control? My dad was strong; why wasn't I. It didn't take many sessions before my therapist told me I was suffering from compassion fatigue and depression. Initially, I thought she was accusing me of not caring and being like those we came across in the hospital. Once I understood this better, we were suffering from a similar problem in a lot of ways. Compassion fatigue is a term that describes the physical, emotional, and psychological impact of helping others, often through experiences of stress or trauma. In my case, I had experienced multiple traumatic events, and it had caught up with me.

It was in some way a blessing in disguise seeing those people at the hospital that had lost their ability to express compassion as I knew I didn't ever want to become like that.

I knew my cup was full and overflowing, I needed to find a way to empty some of it

I started by making discrete changes in my day as initially, I knew my mind couldn't focus for long. I began with just one minute of silence (meditation if you prefer) each morning. I took several deep breaths and sat in silence, and at the end, I included an affirmation for the day; either 'I am strong', 'I am focused', 'I am ok' or others similar.

I was using the flower in the garden moment as a reminder that even little moments of joy can make all the difference. I started what became a healthy daily practice and, without knowing it, a turning point.

Letting go and turning my life around

Reminding myself what I had learnt many years prior, I began the process of learning to let go of the things that I believed were hurting me the most. For me, that was the fear that my family could never be happy again. I had convinced myself that somehow, we deserved this suffering and pain. Once I acknowledged this fear and took a closer look at it, I knew that what I was telling myself had no objective evidence or truth. From there, I worked on finding even the most minor thing to be happy with each day. Introducing a new positive daily habit was the start of a new journey. I began by reaching out to my younger son more often. He had moved interstate to start university two weeks after his brother's injury, so he was alone and suffering. He and his brother are extremely close; they are best mates. Initially, I tried not to dwell on his pain or my husband's; focusing on this would consume me further. They refer to me as the matriarch of the family, as I usually take control and put everyone else's needs before mine – I needed to find a way to do both. I somehow had to get my path sorted, or I would be no use to anyone. Instead, I tried to think about things that bring me joy, like how good it feels when you are being hugged by someone you love – this was something I had been avoiding because I knew my eldest son could not hug me anymore. I ended up compensating for this by over-hugging him, something I am sure he cringes at even now.

While reaching out to my son in Melbourne, I made sure I stayed focused and present as he talked to me about his day. Usually, I would have downloaded his brother's situation and quickly allowed him to update me on his day before hanging up. He also needed his mum and to be reminded how much he was loved and thought about. The best way to describe my youngest son is like a toasted marshmallow, tough on the outside and soft and gooey in the middle. On so many occasions, he has brought the sunshine we have each needed. With his wicked sense of humour, he brightens up the darkest of days. I love him to the moon and back. The same is to be said for my husband, or rather my soulmate. I was so lucky to meet this man and have two amazing boys with him. We have always been in sync, knowing precisely what the other has to say and how they feel. He could see I was withdrawing and needed to do something about it. The doing bit was on me.

Each day I would consciously introduce more things to connect with and focus on, like how I felt when I had my morning coffee, how good it smelled and tasted, and I would take my time to savour each moment. Or how good it felt to have the warmth of the sun on your face. One of the most enjoyable memories was when I would take a friend's two-year-old twins to their swimming lessons. Their laughter would light up the world. It was pure bliss. They lived near the hospital, and I stayed with them for my first few weeks in Sydney. I think about how wonderful that family was and how much I needed their support at the time.

Additional moments included catching up with close friends again, going for a walk in nature, or stopping to listen to the birds in the trees chatting away, or watching the waves roll onto the beach. Each little thing became part of my positive daily ritual to build strength for whatever was coming my way.

> *I included these mindful moments in my journal each day, alongside the pain and anger*

Gradually things shifted from consciously doing these rituals to unconsciously doing them. I looked forward to each of these moments; my senses heightened, I started to smell food again, even better, I could taste food again. Apparently, for some people losing your sense of taste or smell can happen if you are experiencing stress or anxiety. It certainly was the case for me. Very slowly, the pieces were connecting; I wanted to feel again; I had been numb for too long.

Our habits, good or otherwise influence every aspect of our lives

More and more, I used the compass in my journal to build up the pieces of my life. From the details I captured, I could see where the gaps were, where I tried to focus. Over time these small changes were the building blocks that became my new story and ultimately influenced turning my life around. On reflection, I realised that I couldn't have done it if I had attempted a dramatic shift, like a short boot camp or a weekend retreat. The key was to start by changing minor aspects of my daily ritual or routine from filling my days with dread, hurt, and sadness to filling it with joy, connection, and meaning. Once I was ready, I did some weekend retreats and boot camps, and they did wonders for me.

Lifelong goals

During the next few months, I found myself with the capacity to do more, my mind was becoming clear enough to focus, so I embarked on lifelong goals that I had put off. One was to complete my quest to find the family that was stolen from us two generations earlier. Another to grow my business and write this book. And, above all, I would continue to be there for my family and friends.

Solving the puzzle pieces of my past was an incredible experience, and I was only sad that my mum wasn't with me to share it when it happened. As I mentioned earlier, it was a significant change and awkward in a lot of ways. I've always questioned some of our family beliefs about our indigenous heritage, and when I finished discovering my past and seeing all the pieces come together, I initially felt betrayed.

Discovering the incredible journeys of my grandmother and great-grandmothers was surreal. My grandmother was taken from her family when she was only three and placed with 'white' families to be raised white. Her story alone is heartbreaking as she struggled to understand where she truly belonged. Returning home to a family she no longer knew wasn't an option, and she was not white enough to fit in.

They were strong, courageous women each with their own story of survival

My great-great-grandmother seems to have been a real character who wouldn't have put up with much. I liked her already. She had a reputation for taking charge, and even a cheeky ballad was written about her. I believe both she and my great aunt appear in the Stockman's Hall of Fame for their role as stockmen at Brunette Downs Station. To survive, they were forced to adapt and work for the European settlers who took their lands. How incredible it would have been to know them. I felt a sense of connection and loss to my past.

Why had we missed out on this growing up? I knew so little about my mum's family, yet it is half of who I am. It didn't take me long to reframe my thoughts and remind myself that this wasn't about blame; it was about rejoicing in my discovery. Today I fully embrace my entire family history and continue my journey to understand better our indigenous ancestors and the incredible culture we have all missed out on experiencing. For instance, knowing my totem would have been brilliant. Totems are animals, plants, or features of the land that have a special significance or relationship to a person or group. My ancestral and family group totems include the lizard, snake, wallaby, and fly, from what I understand. It just so happens that I had adopted a spirit animal (the turtle) well before I knew about my ancestors.

Returning home with a new identity

Coming home did not resolve all the problems we sustained in the hospital. We soon understood that the hospital was only the beginning. We went from being a 'mainstream' functional family to being part of a minority group who had to fight every step of the way to be heard and treated with respect.

We did not believe we were different people, but apparently, not everyone agreed. We had friends and family who avoided us and a community environment that suddenly appeared disabled in its design. There was bureaucratic red tape to cut through for everything from accessible parking permits to adaptable living arrangements.

The scariest part was taking on the responsibility for our son's health. We weren't medically trained to handle many things that go haywire with a spinal cord injury. As much as aspects of the hospital scared us, strangely, it also provided comfort. The first couple of months at home were highly challenging for all of us. As soon as something happened, I tried not to panic, but I had no choice at times. Everything they said in the handbook that my son could experience somehow arrived at our door in the first 12 months. The good news is, we can now speak SCI (spinal cord injury) language and take any new issue in our stride. Well, almost, a recent unfortunate change in our son's health has put us all back on notice, but that is a story for another time. We eventually found a routine, and I found my resolve to remain calm and confident to do this. I've seen some gory stuff, and let's just say, watching horror movies is now a breeze.

Outside the home, we had more significant hurdles to overcome. We met plenty of people who felt they had a cure for our son's paralysis. He was offered up everything from just believing that he could walk to special potions, crystals, and the best of all, a simple touch from a Scientologist, who was also a disability taxi driver. Despite their best intentions, these cures fell somewhat short. My son is a realist and is committed to keeping going whilst maintaining hope that medical research might have the answer one day.

Disabled by design

A word of advice for anyone designing or building accessible constructions, including pathways, you might want to sit in a wheelchair or use a Zimmer frame to test if it works first. The number of properties we looked at that were advertised as 'accessible' were anything but. One had a step down into the front door; others were located on the second floor with no lift access, umm! Recently we booked accommodation that was located across from a hospital where the website stated accessible rooms; great if you could first get past the three steps into the building. Even simply crossing the road had become a hazard with kerb and gutters not being the same height. You can never assume all café and restaurant tables are adjustable either; we made that mistake more than once. Nowadays, we call ahead to confirm.

Being my father's daughter and armed with the character and courage from my ancestors' stories inspired me to remain resilient and never give up fighting for our place back in the community. I'm guessing because of this; there are probably dart boards inside some organisations with my name on them.

The best way to describe the experience was like arriving on Mars and figuring out how to survive.

> *We were suddenly aliens, and people around us were stepping aside to avoid any contact*

One of the most significant changes was having to organise carers for my son. We had converted our garage to an accessible living space to move back into; however, he now needed 24-hour care. This was my first introduction to the world of disability care, and I must say it was a real eye-opener. We interviewed several organisations before settling on a couple. The ironic part was that my son was doing disability care work to put him through university before his injury. It was probably fortunate to have some inside knowledge, and this was ultimately why he did not want his parents to become his full-time carers. We worked through the trials of finding suitable carers, and I must say the care team my son has today is terrific. We all adore them.

These were the challenging parts; we had the most incredible support from other individuals on the flip side.

Expressing gratitude and being mindful

My sister and my son's girlfriend provided respite at the hospital when my husband and I needed a break. Dear friends and family rallied together to raise funds so we could renovate our house, others organised the renovation, we were sent care packages, and there was always someone reaching out to check on us, and they still do.

As a family, our way of handling stress was to take turns razzing each other up; this odd sort of humour was how we supported each other and kept us all on the hook for coping together. We are not shy about having tough conversations, and we always manage to find something to laugh about.

> *I will be forever grateful for the kindness and support we received*

I finally accepted that we had all changed from this experience, and we were now adapting to a new way of living. My son carries the change load; however, we also needed to adapt to ensure all our lives continued to have the meaning of his family. I now include carer in my job description. Although this is not something I do daily, I still consider myself a primary carer for my son as needing others to help with his physical needs is his new norm. Therefore, the role of a carer is also our new norm.

Thinking back, I felt some of my shame about how I may have been before my son's injury. Was I kind enough or understanding enough of other people's situations? I'd like to believe I was understanding. However, most of us can only observe and assume we know life from another person's perspective. I realise that you cannot fully appreciate another's journey unless you have had the same or similar experience. I am incredibly mindful of this and use it as my guide to making better decisions and fewer judgements. I try to see the situation through a different lens, a walk-in their shoes or a wheel in their chair.

Grit over pain and anger

Initially, I thought writing a book about our harrowing ordeal would be the ultimate healing adventure. I wrote 270 pages of pain, anger, and anguish, but I could not bring myself to do anything with that book in the end because it was not who I was, and I did not want to be a victim and be forever remembered for that experience.

Despite not changing the hospital environment or influencing an entire community, many things have been resolved since those nine difficult months in the hospital. Our family members are now stronger individuals, and we try to align ourselves with kind and compassionate individuals who, like us, want to live in a world where everyone matters.

My youngest son is the most motivated, resilient, inspiring young man I've ever known. Of course, I am biased. He is about to become a qualified landscaper; he purchased his first property during the pandemic and fully renovated it in lockdown. Well, I did advise on the colour scheme via zoom. Despite how much he was hurting, being alone in another state away from the family he loves and his adored brother, my son continues to remind us how amazing he is. He is the first to step in and help those around him, being available for a chat (worse than my dad), a laugh and a joke to keep us all going. I'm so proud of the incredible person he has become.

I'm also very proud of my eldest son, who now lives independently with his partner. He continues to explore different work and study options whilst writing brilliant lyrics. I often wonder if he is thinking about becoming a rapper! He has always been good with words; I tried to convince him to do this book for me. He is the most like my dad, with extraordinary courage, wise beyond his years, and such a calming influence on others. Each day he learns more about how to survive and thrive living with a spinal cord injury. The mental load he carries from having such an injury takes its toll same days; that is where we all work together to pull him through. I know now more than ever that being able to protect him with a great cover story like the one about the apple in his tummy when he was three isn't going to cut it as an adult. Watching him take on this enormous challenge and yet still give so much of himself to those around him humbles me. When he was a disability support worker, his clients adored him. To the point that when some of them found out that he was injured, they made the journey to Sydney to visit him. He has always been an incredibly kind and compassionate human; that is why it hurt so much when he wasn't always shown kindness when he needed it most.

He has a long road ahead of him and continues to battle with his health; the sad part about this type of injury; things can be significantly more complex. If there were a way to trade places with him, I would do it instantly, but life doesn't work like that; each of us must play the hand we are dealt. I know he is strong enough and loved enough to take this journey and find the answers he needs to live his best life.

We will be there for each other, no matter what

Remarkably, my husband and I remain together. What's the saying; what doesn't kill you makes you stronger? That certainly describes our eventful life together thus far. There are times when I wonder how we keep going, yet we always manage to find our way through. He is another motivated person with a great sense of humour, which saved us more than once. As soon as he would arrive at the hospital on a Friday afternoon, he would have my son and me laughing within minutes, allowing us some needed respite from another long week. Just days before Christmas 2018, he was hit by a car and knocked off his bike. Up until that moment, I thought this man was invincible, and I relied on him so much for us to get through. He had broken his clavicle and needed surgery, and thankfully he made a full recovery;

however, it was a stark reminder of how vulnerable each of us is. After three decades together, we remain the best of friends, always there for each other and our family. The results are two incredible sons and everlasting love and respect.

Each day I start with the intention of having a great day; when I greet people, and they ask how I am, I say, 'I'm wonderful'. This small ritual makes a huge difference and helps if things turn ugly, as my positivity somehow reduces the impact and ensures I don't fall into too dark a place. Having a quirky sense of humour isn't a bad backup either.

Although I plan, I don't look too far ahead; I spend more time enjoying the present. I thoroughly enjoy my work and meeting wonderful people in the process. I know a few key milestones will fill me with joy, meet my future grandchildren (no pressure boys), and find a moment to properly celebrate our son's significant 21st and 18th birthday and the many other milestones that we missed.

I consciously seek joy and try to find happy moments for myself

Our new norm often comes with complex challenges; we try to tackle them together as they arise. I still go into meltdown on occasion, especially when I come across sheer incompetence, but overall, I am doing remarkably well. Additionally, I volunteer my time to help some of our most vulnerable citizens, who struggle to work through bureaucratic red tape, ensure they have a voice and get their most basic needs met. Today, I am pretty different from who I was before my son's accident, and my rituals, beliefs, and values continue to evolve. I try not to sweat the small stuff, and instead, I shrug my shoulders and carry on. Allowing joy in and not feeling guilty about being happy is the most significant shift for me.

People who know me know that I am genuine; I'm always ready to offer up a smile and to lend a hand to help others. Apart from calling poor behaviour when I see it, I actively seek ways to be kinder to each other.

I try to listen without judgement

Many people look at our family and think we are incredibly resilient and strong because of what we have experienced and what we continue to live through. They comment on our sense of humour, humility, and compassion for others, and they wonder why we are not angry and broken. We are not damaged or mad because we choose not to be. We probably understand better than most how fragile life is, and, as such, we want to live our best lives possible, full of hope and joy. At times I have family or friends say they feel guilty when they talk about their problems, suggesting they are insignificant compared to ours. The greatest lesson I have learned is that everyone experiences some level of stress, trauma, or significant change throughout their lives. Yet each of our experiences is unique, and the way we handle things will be different, and that is okay. Comparing yourself to others is not only a waste of time; it can be harmful. What is essential is finding your way again and, therefore, why **Navigate beyond Now** was created.

By committing to letting go of my fears and making small changes, using my compass to check in on what mattered most to me helped in so many ways. I was so fixated on one element in my life that I had forgotten almost anyone and anything else. It was essential to remedy this for me to function and to be happy. My diary has become an incredible resource for my family, for my healing' and for days when I feel like we cannot possibly take any more bad news. I look back through it and see how far we have already come. I know if we have done it before, we can do it again.

When thinking about those dark times at the hospital and loved ones being lost or injured, I realised I had also lost my way at some point. Strangely I could relate to those I accused of being indifferent, detached.

We are all impacted by our experiences; they are the very essence of who we become. I didn't realise that I had a choice in how my experiences, good or bad, would influence my life.

Facing some old fears

Recently my son needed to return to the hospital in Sydney for another major surgery. He was terrified at how he might be treated, and the memories from the past soon flooded back in to haunt him.

It turned out that this experience was vastly different. Firstly, the surgery went well, yeah! And secondly, the culture on the ward had changed. I was oddly thankful he got to experience this again so that he might one day be able to replace the experiences of the past with more positive ones.

It would have been easy to allow my own horrible experiences to dictate my future and become the anchor I use to excuse my behaviour, or I could choose another path. I know the person I want to be and remain; I just got lost for a while, hence the need for my compass to set me back on my path.

On reflection

I am now in a place where I can reflect on each of these events and talk through a process for how I coped; at the time, I was a mess just going through the motions to get through each day. Irrespective of the many tragic circumstances we have endured, we are still vulnerable to whatever might come next. The only difference is we have some idea of how painful it can be. Every time a loved one is hurt or suffering, we feel it like it is the first time. The pain is all-consuming and leaves very little room for coping. Sure, some people do suppress their emotions to protect themselves, but this comes at a price. When you construct barriers or suppress your feelings, you can become withdrawn, less communicative, and potentially lose your way. Having the courage to confront these things honestly is crucial if your compass points 'true'.

Introducing a daily ritual of small positive change helped me have greater connection and control over my life.

As I coach clients to navigate their work and life changes, I am constantly reminded of my journey and choices. Although I have the skills to guide and support others, I'm not responsible for their direction or decisions.

We are each on our unique journey; we have our own story to create. What will your story be? What direction will you take?

Work lessons

Here is an entirely different story. It looks at my working environment, but I hope you will see how this theme is related to what I am talking about regarding our decisions, attitudes, and behaviours.

Let me begin with how my previous work experiences have influenced the way I work today.

My colourful career

I have worked both for myself and some of Australia's largest private enterprises, not-for-profits, small businesses, and several Government appointments throughout my career. I have met some interesting characters and experienced a variety of workplace cultures. In my early working years, the late 1980s and early 1990s, I was exposed to deplorable behaviours, including sexism, racism, rewarding poor performance, bullying and harassment in the workplace, and poor leadership. At the time, I was not shocked by it, as it was part of the culture of that era. There was no political correctness or social media to track every moment of one's life. Some extremes for me included being propositioned to gain a promotion, interviewed by men in private hotel rooms, frequently offered drugs by my supervisors and colleagues, and expected to spend 'weekends away' with the boss. The weirdest was the number of times I was caught at what seemed like social gatherings with colleagues but ended up being platforms to peddle pyramid selling schemes. I'll be honest, Amway and I didn't gel. Sales full stop was not my strong point.

You could say I was a bit naïve back then. However, it did not take long for me to realise what was being asked of me and that I had a choice, and I learnt to push back and stand up for myself. At the time, my responses did impact my career opportunities, as I was often being overlooked in favour of others with less experience. It toughened me up, though, and I soon learnt to speak up or be left behind. As my confidence grew, my outlook towards work opened many doors in my life and career. I became known for identifying misalignment within organisations, connecting people, and building positive working relationships to improve outcomes and influence the culture.

Despite feeling like the workplace therapist, I used my talent to move into roles that further expanded these skills.

I mentioned above that in those days you expected to see some poor behaviour like bullying and big egos within a workplace, unfortunately. However, time does not seem to have eliminated this kind of behaviour. Below I'll walk you through some more recent work experiences that my clients and I have witnessed. You will be surprised that not only do we continue to put up with toxic culture, we sometimes reward the behaviour. This is what ultimately pushed me into reassessing my career.

Leadership lessons

As a professional change manager, my role is to assess an organisation's readiness for change, provide an approach to implement successful transition, and coach leaders to bring their people along the journey. I need to be clear about the strategic direction, leadership, and culture of an organisation to be effective. Doing this role, I have had the pleasure of working for some of the most incredible leaders, as well as the misfortune of working for some horrible ones. I have witnessed male and female managers who were happy to shame and humiliate staff in front of others and, on many occasions, reduce individuals to tears. On the other hand, I've seen influential leaders in action. Honestly, it's a game-changer. You are so drawn in by their ability to remain calm, act and drive an environment that nurtures and develops people to become their best.

I remember one exceptional leader. She understood people and what she needed to do to get them to buy into the organisation's direction, and she asked for their input and led from there.

Her key leadership qualities included the attributes of an effective team coach

There was never any ambiguity about where the organisation was headed or the use of fear tactics to drive outcomes; everyone felt like they had been heard and were a part of the bigger picture. Everyone was engaged and energised to be part of her team, and the environment matched the tone. That was effective leadership in action.

I have recently watched several individuals being promoted to leadership roles who frankly are not ready to lead. Often these promotions were a way of moving people aside for poor performance or reacting to fill a void. These decisions concern me as I have seen plenty of examples of the effects these decisions can have on an organisation and the significant impact on culture.

Some of my clients have witnessed or been part of this type of decision-making from the top, and they come to me looking for a way out. Sadly, they are often brilliant operators, yet their leaders do not see what should be obvious.

Unless you are prepared to invest in developing and understanding your people or yourself to be an effective leader, you can't expect to achieve success. The performance of an organisation sits squarely on the shoulders of those leading and driving the culture.

I remember being asked to manage an underperforming team and make some tough decisions about the team's future. Once I did some unpacking, I soon discovered that the leaders before me hadn't invested the time into developing their team, leaving them behind their colleagues in performance. In the end, I decided to invest in those that wanted to remain and found more suitable positions for those not ready to evolve, achieving the best outcome for all.

Leadership includes making tough decisions; however, if you ensure your people are at the centre of your decision making, they will trust you are making them for the right reasons. Reactive leadership does not instil confidence. How do you expect to lead and develop others if you are not shown to lead or have poor role models?

I keep in contact with some of my favourite leaders, and they continue to mentor me and remind me what is effective leadership. I use any learnings they impart in my work when coaching and developing others.

My takeaway message from all of them is, **to lead is to listen, act and continually evolve.**

Spinning my wheels

Several years ago, I found myself spinning my wheels at work and didn't feel engaged in what I was doing. By this time, I was earning a healthy income, and I was considered an expert in my field, yet this didn't seem to be enough for me. I struggled to work in environments with ineffective leadership and toxic cultures, which took a toll on other aspects of my life. I did not fully appreciate the effect these environments had on my life until I sat down to check in on where

I was headed. I used the life balance sheet included in part two of this book as a guide to see how things were stacking up, what I had accomplished and what was holding me back.

> *Essentially, what was important to me in the workplace was the piece that was missing*

At times, you get caught up in the humdrum of daily work life, and before you know it, you become part of the culture you were trying to fix. It becomes a ritual or habit you can't break. You find yourself working at cross purposes to your beliefs and values.

Aligning my values, changing my behaviour

Like everyone else, we take mental notes of what we like and don't like based on our interactions, education, and experiences as we go through life's journey. From these experiences, we build a picture of who we want to become using these reference points to inform our values and beliefs.

We also form our behaviours or habits based on these experiences; some are positive habits and others not. For me, I fell into the same working routine, bought into the culture around me, even though I knew it went against my values. Using my life compass, I validated my gaps and realised that I needed to embark on a different path that was more aligned to my current values.

> *It was time to look at the problem from a different perspective*

The working environments I found myself in didn't fit my needs anymore. It was more than that. I knew I still had a passion for the type of work; I just needed to do it differently and in environments ready for what I was offering.

Changing tack

After realising I needed to change tack, I decided I needed a plan. It started with enrolling into some further study about human behaviours, effective leadership, our habits, and what affects our well-being. I needed to understand more about our idiosyncrasies and how each of us is wired.

At the same time, I researched organisations with known effective leadership and notably collaborative workplace environments. I wanted to understand why they were so successful, what were they doing differently.

The key elements I discovered from the top rating organisational cultures I researched were that they all had a clear direction and aligned leadership. They were innovative and inclusive environments, and above all, their people were their priority.

> *Don't be afraid to recognise when something isn't working and to act upon it*

With the knowledge I gained from the additional study and research, I decided to turn my attention to growing my own business and designed a new role for myself without giving up what I loved. I had run businesses of my own before and realised that this is where I was at my best.

Today I enter an organisation with an improved mindset. Although I'm no longer an employee, I still need to ensure I'm doing good work and achieving results. With my adjusted approach and thinking, I continue to assess the environment, culture, and structure and provide honest, practical advice to leaders on what is achievable based on where they are today. The difference is I no longer allow myself to get pulled into the politics of an organisation or fall into poor workplace habits; I try to remain true to myself and my objectives.

Maybe this will come as a surprise to you, but the part about being honest was vital for me. In some previous engagements, I was pressured by my bosses or the team around me not to update management on what they needed to know but rather tell them what they believed and wanted to hear. This never sat well with me. Hence why I was disengaged, and the reason why I eventually started my own business. I began with a set of core values, including **Trust**, **Authenticity**, **Accountability**, **Empathy**, and **Equality**. These values remain the same today.

In part two of this book, you will get to work on values and beliefs using your compass.

The influence of our basic needs

In the past, I had made choices to work in organisations that did not necessarily align with my values, as the need to earn a living—won out. For instance, If I didn't believe in mining, working for an organisation like Rio Tinto would go against my values. However, if I needed to earn money and this was the only choice at the time, I would need to make a choice.

Later in this book, I have a section about **our basic needs** and how people will generally prioritise these facets in their lives above everything else (including our values).

We might pause here for a moment and use the COVID-19 pandemic as a real example of how we pursue our most basic needs above everything else. When word of the pandemic spread, supermarket shelves became depleted as households stocked up on essentials. People used social media to post best buys on meat, deep freezers, toilet paper, hand sanitiser, and many other 'essential' items. As humans, we are instinctively triggered by a fight or flight response to an event perceived as stressful or frightening. We are programmed to react to ensure our immediate (basic) needs are being met. It is usually during a crisis or similar that we put ourselves and these needs above all else. Hence, some of the crazy news stories we saw with people fighting over the last rolls of toilet paper and the like. These reactions will continue to play out until we feel safe in the knowledge that all is well again.

Another unfortunate example of how the imbalance of our basic needs can impact our lives was when I became aware of a person who had lost their house in a fire. The home was underinsured, and the man didn't have the means to access more funds, so he resorted to misappropriating funds from his workplace. The result was devasting as not only did the family lose their home, but he also now had a criminal record.

When elements of our basic needs are missing, the result could be like the more extreme examples of the ones above, or it could be something more subtle, like your inability to focus on work due to a lack of sleep or poor nutrition. This was true for me at the time of my son's injury, when I barely slept, which had a significant impact on my ability to focus on work entirely.

Think about a work situation where your basic needs may have influenced your behaviour or challenged your values?

Are you ready for the truth and to act?

Influential leaders will always want to hear the truth and be ready to make decisions.

Unfortunately, some leaders are not always ready to hear the truth about what is going on in their organisation. A funny man I once worked with articulated it like this, 'they're not ready to hear their baby is ugly'. On many occasions, I was expected to wave my magic change wand and hey presto, the culture is improved, productivity is up, and employees are happy.

> *Someone who delegates accountability is not a leader*

This message holds true for a lot of us, not just ineffective bosses. I have been guilty of avoiding feedback that I am not ready to face. The difference for leaders is they have a responsibility for the organisation they run and the people they lead.

Among those I worked with, the leaders who demonstrated maturity and professional competence were the ones who were willing to own the reality of the status quo, including the culture. They took accountability and accepted what needed to be done to transform effectively. When this happens, you get to witness true change success and have cause for celebration. Once a leader can clearly define their problem, lead from the front, be accountable and act, and inspire the workforce to support them, you have a winning formula. These are the organisations I try to seek out to work with today.

The organisations that I used to spend time trying to convince and drag along had leaders who were still hanging on to blame and pointing the finger at everyone else but themselves. I have this message for these organisations; **the fish rots from the head down. Until you learn to be accountable for your actions, you will fail to evolve.**

Speaking of accountability, we've all been in a position where we have made a mistake. Sometimes we just get things wrong. We are only human, so there will be errors; they don't call it 'human error' for nothing. The issue is how we react when we make a mistake. All too often, we duck for cover and try to either sweep it under the carpet or, better still, pin it on someone else.

I have so many examples of this happening that they would fill a book on its own. I've seen issues from losing files to losing millions and everything in between with zero accountability taken. Some of the more memorable excuses of what went wrong were, let's say, newsworthy. I'm sure you can all think of when you have seen this type of behaviour and cringed.

If you make a mistake, own it. It's empowering to know you are brave enough to admit when you are wrong. Blame should only be reserved for those that do not know better.

Your wellbeing in the workplace

Over the years, I have seen many talented people leave their jobs or become unwell at work because of the toxic culture. It is called toxic culture for a reason; it damages people.

Some people don't feel they have a choice to leave, or other more compelling reasons force them to stay in their jobs, leaving them to put up with poor culture. Others are worried their career prospects will be limited if they go, so instead continue to complain about what is happening around them yet stay silent.

The lesson I learned from the saying, 'You are a product of your environment, was finding working environments aligned with my values. Otherwise, I would spend the remainder of my career swimming against the current, or worse, it could impact your health. When checking in on my life compass, I realised my work was affecting my well-being.

The cost of workplace stress in Australia as of 2020 was nearly 15 billion dollars. That is not because of the pandemic; that is a consistent figure that is only growing.

The reaction to push staff to seek help or access programs like EAP (employee assistance programs) is excellent if that is what the individual needs; however, we are failing to look at the root cause, and often that lies within the organisation's culture itself.

I've always been surprised by the amount of money organisations pour into staff assistance programs and absorb the increasing number of absenteeisms and yet spend very little on improving the actual culture.

> *The wellbeing of a workplace matters, we all need to invest in it*

An all too familiar example of a toxic workplace is when staff no longer talk to each other directly to resolve issues or ask questions—preferring to hide behind an email or resorting to avoidance behaviour. Bitching about your colleagues around the water cooler is not cool. Try having a good old conversation with the person you are concerned about; you might be surprised at the results. Often, it is generally the first time they've heard of there being an issue. Talk more to each other. It's that simple. Say hello each day and check in on your teammates to see if they are ok. We are a long time working, wouldn't it be nice if we were kinder to each other. Try it; it can't hurt.

Culture is the character and personality of an organisation. When it's healthy, you can feel it. Employees want to stay, others want to join, performance and satisfaction levels are generally high, and effective leadership drives the positive culture. For me, the workplace is an extension of who I am and what I represent. Over the years, many of my colleagues have come up with exciting nicknames for me; **little miss sunshine, Mary Poppins, the disco ball, and the glue that joins people together.** I'm honoured that they saw me this way.

Observing the kind and dedicated staff, like those that supported my son when he needed it most, and the many others I've had the privilege of working with is all the role modelling I needed to know which workplace environment I wanted to be in.

Stop following other poor behaviours and start discovering what works for you. Be brave

Healthy workplace culture goes beyond good leadership; it includes collaboration and communication, purpose and aligned values, trust, effective teamwork, building positive relationships, and doing meaningful work. All these aspects influence your behaviour and attitude towards others at work and in your life. Working with or putting up with bullies or poor behaviour only incites and reinforces the behaviour. You would be surprised how many people are not even aware of their behaviour and how it affects others.

What do you want your colleagues to say about you? We all remember the bully from school; this is the same in the workplace. You do have the choice to change your behaviour and take the higher ground. Sure, it can be difficult sometimes, and sometimes you feel alone in your mission; however, you need to be seen modelling positive behaviours to affect positive change.

Being part of an unhealthy culture at work will eventually catch up with you and affect you far beyond the office walls. The next time you are in the office, ask yourself if your workplace is healthy; decide what you can do differently if the answer is no.

I learnt the hard way by burning myself out trying to convince others to be kinder or take accountability for their actions; in the end, the only one that changed was me, and not in a good way.

Using an approach like the letter I wrote to the hospital on behalf of my son and how I conduct my business today, I don't need to convince anyone; I make them aware of the problem, and they can decide what they choose to do about it.

Be true to yourself

Remember, each of us is different. Your values and beliefs will be different from mine. You may find that you completely disagree with my approach to my work. That is the point. You need to be able to define your path to fulfilment.

> *Modelling the behaviour you expect from others is the quickest way to influence your work culture and the community around you*

Starting my own business was scary, but what worked for me. Today, I continue to focus on helping organisations and individuals manage and master change, although I do it with essential values. By being honest without judgement, I can guide others to make a difference for themselves and their organisations. I share the skills and knowledge required to master the art of change by rethinking our habits and shifting our mindsets. Clients engage me as they appreciate my candour, enthusiasm, and openness. I challenge them and provide professional, practical advice to help them through their journeys.

My past experiences have led me to this point and have shaped my character, values, beliefs and ideas, and attitude.

It's your turn

I'm sharing my story and giving you your compass to work on in the hope that you will also get the opportunity to discover more about the person you want to be. I hope my experience shows that we can pick up the pieces and redefine ourselves; we need to take the first step.

Remember, these are my examples of elements in all our lives – work, home, community, health, etc. Each of those can affect how we react and behave.

As you have purchased this book, I am guessing you are either stuck and need a nudge, experiencing some difficulty, or ready to evaluate aspects of your own life and check that you align with your actual values. A key question will arise for you: **'what are you prepared to change or challenge to ensure you are getting the most out of life?'**

This book is a tool to 'check in' on where you are today and where you want to be based on the choices you make. I could have chosen to remain angry and hurt by some of my experiences; however, this would have negatively affected my entire life. Instead, I decided to learn from my experiences and help others by offering simple life messages on resetting intentions and becoming the best version of oneself, no matter the circumstances.

It is never too late to reevaluate your life. What will you choose to do differently?

Use this book as a prompt to guide you through your journey. It will help you to find your true-life compass and to realise your full potential.

What are you waiting for ... begin

Part two
Your compass

This section is your compass or wellbeing guide. It is yours to refer to, write in, critique or update. The intent is broad and holistic. It is not meant to be focused on a single element (e.g., a workplace or a personal tragedy); these were my examples of how life can unfold to get you thinking about your journey.

The activities included throughout are meant to be thought-provoking and hopefully give you a nudge to get you started in another direction. Some you will relate to more than others; the key is discovering the elements that resonate with you as these become your tools for success.

I would recommend working through the book from the beginning, using the roadmap as a guide. However, there is no wrong approach. There are several types of compasses used in this book; a life compass, one to check in on your happiness, your daily needs, and others marked Status updates; these are to track your progress if you have set some goals or are working on new habits. Speaking of habits, did you know journaling is a great mindful habit to lift your mood. You will undoubtedly get plenty of opportunities to practice that here.

When I initially put this book together, it was based on my journal from our hospital stay and some of my professional workplace coaching techniques. From there, it grew into what you see today.

Our team of change influencers have helped with the insights included in this section based on their coaching success. The idea was to provide a product that anyone could pick up and start using as a self-guide to improve their wellbeing. My business provides professional coaching services; however, not everyone can afford one-on-one coaching, so we evolved our service to include a group coaching service or this compass as a self-coaching option. A part of our core values is to ensure anyone looking for coaching support can access these tools.

Throughout the book, you will find many of my affirmations as well as quotes from others. Please capture your thoughts on these pages and note whether you agree or disagree with the message. I chose to deliver my message this way because I wanted you to understand that I am just an ordinary person who has experienced some extraordinary moments in life and come out the other side relatively okay.

I've read some profound life experiences from both unknown individuals to celebrities. Some of these stories include miracle solutions for whatever it is you are going through. The reality is nobody has a miracle cure for anyone else's circumstances. You are the only one that can decide which way you want to go. I have learned enough to know how to seek some answers, and I also know what it takes to develop the skills needed to be resilient, adaptable, and motivated to set your life compass on the right path. The rest is up to you.

Feedback on how practical this book is would be much appreciated; after all, I am also on a journey to become my best self. The best way to provide feedback is via my website www.bespokechange.com.au. This site includes information on building your life compass, changing habits, and managing change.

Maria

You've got this

We are all visitors to this time, this place. We are just passing through. Our purpose here is to observe, to learn, to grow, to love… and then we return home.

Australian Aboriginal Proverb

Begin

Begin

Start now; you will never have more time than you do right now. Write the first thing that comes to you, then use this page to remind yourself what you thought when you began.

One day or day one. It is your decision.
Unknown

Journey through life

As a journey is a common metaphor for life, I've used this to help you to navigate. We start where we are, figure out where we want to head, ensure we have what we need to succeed, be ready to adjust as we go, as sometimes our plans change.

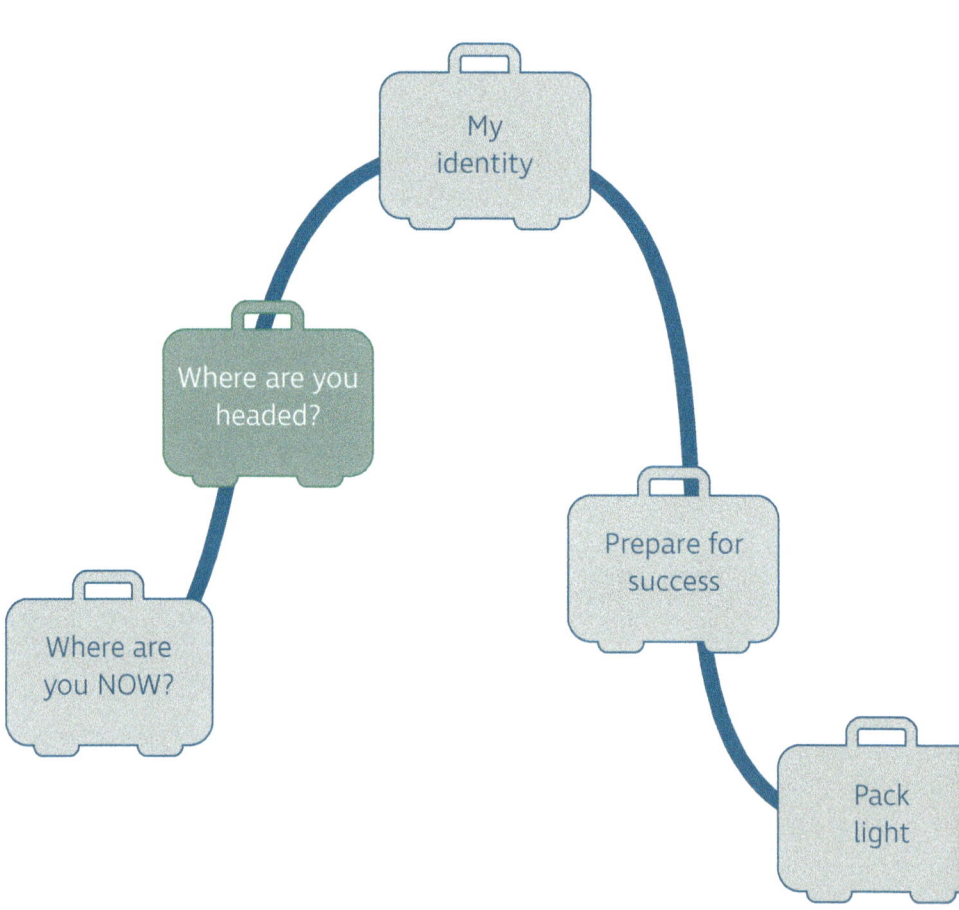

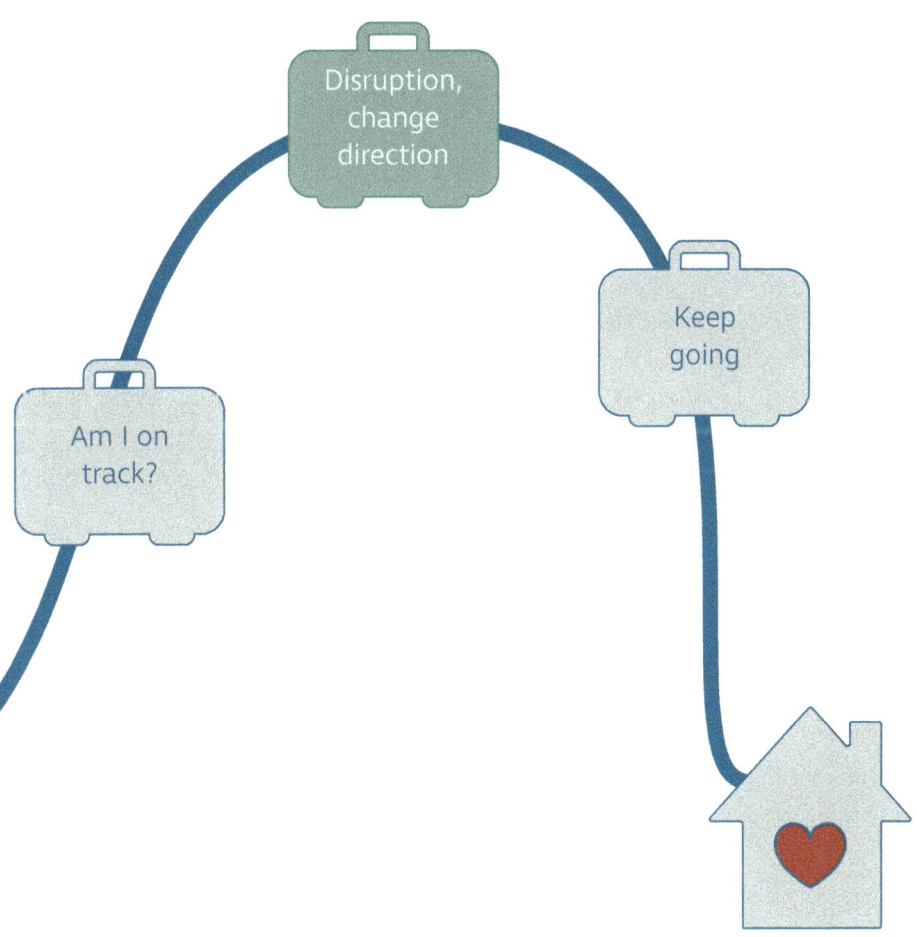

Let's start by checking in on your wellbeing. Using your life compass you will discover where you are now and where you would like to be.

My wellbeing

There is a lot of talk about our wellbeing and trying to improve it, yet most of us still do not understand what is meant by wellbeing.

The **Oxford Dictionary** defines wellbeing as **the state of being comfortable, healthy, or happy. How you feel about yourself and your life.**

It's a bit more complex than this. Many factors affect our wellbeing, including lifestyle choices, socioeconomics, biological factors, and environmental and societal factors.

Although many external factors are outside our control (like a pandemic), there are several aspects we do have control over, like how we behave and our attitude to life.

Well-being is both subjective and objective, and this journal covers a bit of both (e.g., our health, work, connections, values, and beliefs, and then how we feel each day). Let's check in on where you are now.

So, how is it going?

We are each responsible for our well-being journey. You hold the secret to how it turns out. Believe in your ability to take the steps needed to live your best life.

My life compass

Where is your life compass pointed today?
Using my example here as a guide, draw a diagram that includes the critical aspects of your life (what is important to you), e.g., health, finances, work, knowledge, skills, relationships, security, or home, and how these aspects stack up today. Rate them 0-5 (5 being excellent).

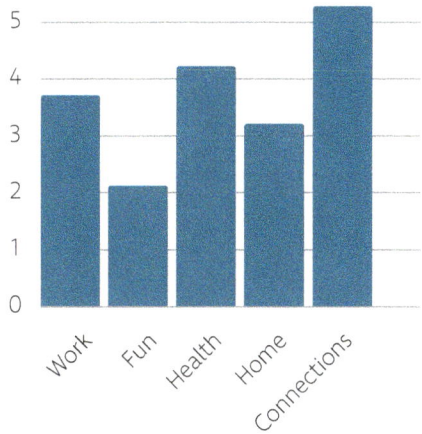

The idea is to understand which aspects in your life are affecting your wellbeing today, including areas that might be holding you back or that need your attention and those aspects that are thriving.

Ensure you look at each category in detail; for instance, **try to include physical, mental,** and spiritual **health** in your assessment. For **work**, think about meaningful activity, challenge, opportunity, environment, leadership, culture.

You can use these aspects or add others you believe are essential to your wellbeing, e.g., serving your community.

My compass today

My compass as at

My ideal compass

Thinking about what is important to you and being realistic about what is possible, what would your ideal life compass look like two years from now? Where should it be pointed to better align with your values? Re-draw your diagram to show how you would like it to look.

Resetting my compass

Which aspect of your 'ideal' compass would you focus on first and why? What will you do to improve this aspect? When will you begin? Use the SMART goal setting to help you get started.

In the first part of this book, I take you through my examples (personal and work) of what I did to make changes based on where I was at the time.

Decide and act

My multi-year compass

I also made a multi-year view of my life compass, showing the significant difference between, say, 2015, where my work was letting me down, 2017, when my son had his tragic accident, and 2021 finding my way again. This might be something you would like to create to see how things change over time.

Capture your multi-year compass here

You are all you need
to be brilliant.

Daily essentials

Every single one of us needs **each of these elements daily** to set ourselves up for success. Are you getting your basic daily needs?

🥑	Nourishing FOOD for growth and function
🚰	WATER – essential to hydrate and cleanse the body
🏠	Suitable SHELTER for protection from the elements
🌙	6–8 hours of SLEEP
👪	Physical and/or emotional CONNECTION
💻	ACTIVITY to create the opportunity to learn and the potential to fail

Use this as your micro compass to check in with daily. As these elements are being fulfilled, you will soon find space to work on the other aspects included in your life compass.

TIP: print this out and put it on your fridge

A good laugh and a long sleep are the two best cures for anything.

Irish proverb

Listen to your gut;

it knows

what you need.

Happiness is!

There are many studies on happiness, and what makes us happy, you would be surprised at the results. In short, experiences, connections, and the act of giving far outweigh money, possessions, high income or receiving gifts. Finland has been ranked the happiest country globally for the last four years (2021), and work/life balance appears to be their answer.

Write down or draw pictures of what makes you happy. Try to capture at least 20 things that make you happy.

Happiness for me is...

Happiness Check-in

Measuring your happiness can be difficult, so I'll ask a different question, how content are you right now? Thinking about this moment, do you feel like everything is ok, or do you desire something else, or more. Using the guide below, which face best describes how content you are with life now? Record the number, time, and date. Check-in as often as you like. Note if it changes each time.

1   2   3   4

Right now I'm feeling like a ( ) __/__/__ @ __:__

Right now I'm feeling like a ( ) __/__/__ @ __:__

Right now I'm feeling like a ( ) __/__/__ @ __:__

Right now I'm feeling like a ( ) __/__/__ @ __:__

Right now I'm feeling like a ( ) __/__/__ @ __:__

Right now I'm feeling like a ( ) __/__/__ @ __:__

Right now I'm feeling like a ( ) __/__/__ @ __:__

Right now I'm feeling like a ( ) __/__/__ @ __:__

Being happy is on you; your state of mind determines what feels good and what does not.

We are all heading somewhere. When you make specific plans or set some goals it provides greater purpose and meaning, making the journey more exciting and challenging. Let's find out where you are headed.

Where are you headed?

Start with an idea

Knowing where you are headed is difficult without a clearly defined goal. Your life compass will have provided some focus; however, coming up with a plan can be daunting if you don't practice this often. By writing down some of the ideas, dreams, or aspirations in your head, you can start to formulate your goals. You might be thinking, why bother? They're never going to happen. That is precisely the reason to write them down. Never say never. It does not matter how crazy they are. Crazy worked out for these people:

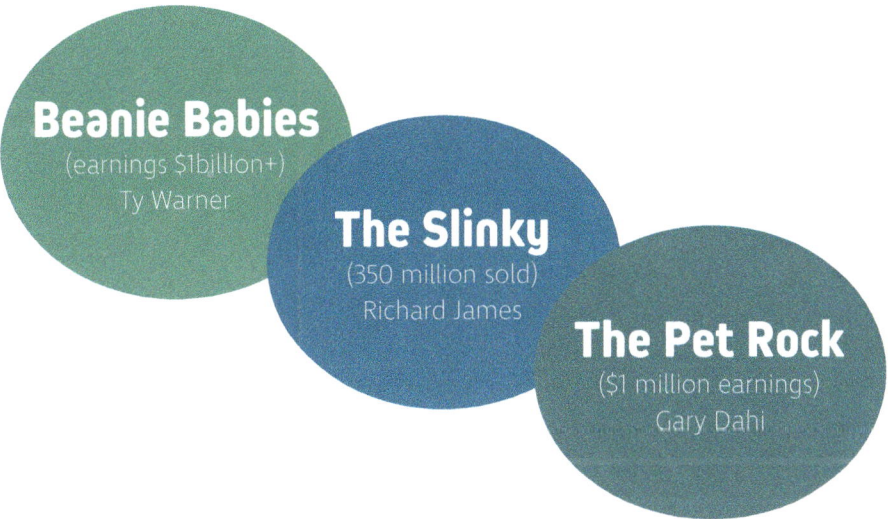

Beanie Babies
(earnings $1billion+)
Ty Warner

The Slinky
(350 million sold)
Richard James

The Pet Rock
($1 million earnings)
Gary Dahl

Not to mention the introduction of **bottled water** and **canned air**. Perhaps you can come up with something that will eliminate bottled water and be good for the environment.

Ideas, dreams, aspirations

The mind that opens to a new idea never returns to its original size.

Albert Einstein, German–American physicist and Nobel Prize winner

Think about the destination

Everyone needs a purpose or a goal to work towards. Goals help you to trigger new behaviours, guide your focus, and help sustain momentum in life.

The key is setting meaningful goals and working your way to achieving them. With the help of neuroplasticity, your brain is clever enough to recognise the need for adaption when you introduce challenges or goals that you strongly desire.

If you have already been working on resetting your compass, changing your habits, you are ready to set other goals and challenge yourself even more. If this is new to you, I recommend beginning with a goal completed in 4-5 weeks. Use ideas from above to help get you started.

Capture your SMART (specific, measurable, achievable, responsible, timely) goals below.

Use the Status updates included in the **Am I on track** section to check your progress.

In the absence of clearly defined goals, we become strangely loyal to performing daily acts of trivia.

Author Unknown

Pursue the goals that add meaning to your life.

My SMART Goals...
(specific, measurable, achievable, responsible, timely)

My SMART Goals...
(specific, measurable, achievable, responsible, timely)

They are your goals. You only let yourself down when you make excuses. Commit and take action.

Enjoy the journey

Now you have your goals (your destination), you need to prepare for the journey. How many stops will you make (milestones) before you reach your destination? How will you celebrate along the way? Have you anticipated any roadblocks, things that might hold you back or delay you from reaching your goal? Use the guide below to establish some milestones to help you achieve your goals. Like changing your habits, start small and build on them.

Remember, life is one big journey, don't forget to celebrate along the way.

Milestone one:
....

Date to achieve:
....

How I will celebrate my achievement:
....
....
....
....

Is there a consequence of not achieving?
....
....
....
....

More milestones

To find yourself, think for yourself

Socrates, Greek philosopher

If you want to be happy, set a goal that commands your thoughts, liberates your energy, and inspires your hopes.

Andrew Carnegie, Scottish-American industrialist and philanthropist

Life doesn't come with a template; you get to design it as you go.

A letter to my future self

Writing a letter to your future self is also helpful when setting goals. It lets you fast forward to imagine how things might turn out based on the goals you have selected. What would you say to your future self? – in five years

Dear me,

A letter to my future self

What would you say to your future self? – in ten years

Dear me,

A letter to my future self

What would you say to your future self? – in 20 years

Dear me,

Use this section to capture who you are, your strenghts, your passions, values, beliefs, character. These are your superpowers for success

Be authentic, show the world who you are.

What is your Avatar?

Draw your Avatar, be as creative as you dare. An Avatar is an icon or figure that you can create to represent yourself. This is a great tool to get to know your colleagues, build relationships, or just have fun.

In my example below, I've included my personality type from **Myers-Briggs** and **DISC**. You can find out your personality type by searching for these and others like them online.

Are you different in different environments (work/play)?

Name: Magic Maz

Role: Change coach

Kryptonite: Routine / Chocolate

Superpower: Time travel

Key connections: Everyone

Personality: INTP / Risk Taker (ID)

My Avatar

My Other Avatar

Moments that matter

Capture your favourite moments or memories of family, friends, work, travel, achievements, etc. What are the key events that have gotten you to this point? Treat it like your memoir if you prefer. I added pictures here, or you could draw something.

Moments that matter

Feeling engaged

Write down the activities that make you feel engaged, moments where you are actively involved in a task and not just observing from the sideline. The task should be challenging yet achievable. These can be work-related activities, hobbies, sports, connecting with family/friends, or other interests.

I feel engaged when...

Find your flow

You will know when you have discovered flow. You are so lost in the moment that it seems like time has slowed, and you feel invincible.

Being fully engaged and energised by something is the concept of flow. The idea of 'flow' was discovered in the 1970s by the Hungarian-American psychologist Professor Mihaly Csikszentmihalyi.

According to Csikszentmihalyi's research, flow is a state in which people are so involved in an activity that nothing else seems to matter; they are **lost in the moment, in the zone.**

The flow state is an optimal state of **intrinsic motivation**, where people are fully immersed in what they are doing.

Go, find your flow.

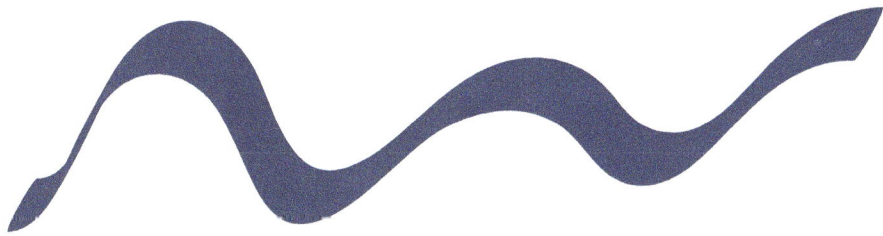

Moments of flow

Write down the moments where you have been 'lost in the moment, so caught up in what you are doing you have lost track of time. Where were you, what were you doing? How did you feel?

Character shows its true colours under pressure or the influence of alcohol.

My secret weapons...

Values—principles or standards of behaviour, one's judgement of what is essential in life.

Character—the mental and moral qualities distinctive to an individual

Beliefs—an acceptance that something exists or is true, especially where there is no proof

VALUES: These are unique to you as an individual. Make a list of your values. What affects or moves you? What is important to you?

CHARACTER: Try the Institute on Character's online character profile survey: https://viacharacter.org/. The survey was developed to help people discover their unique character traits. It is freely available in the public domain and is an excellent resource with lots of data on character traits.

BELIEFS: We have beliefs about ourselves, other people, things, places, events, anything really can be a belief. What are some of your beliefs?

If you struggle to identify your values and beliefs, use the reference list over the page as a prompt.

List of values—this list is not exhaustive; it's just a guide if you need

Family	Respect	Honesty
Freedom	Joy/Play	Adventure
Security	Forgiveness	Kindness
Loyalty	Working Smarter/Harder	Teamwork
Intelligence	Excitement	Career
Connection	Change	Communication
Creativity	Goodness	Learning
Humanity	Involvement	Excellence
Success	Faith	Innovation
Respect	Wisdom	Quality
Invention	Beauty	Commonality
Diversity	Caring	Contributing
Generosity	Personal Development	Spirituality
Integrity	Attitude	Strength
Love	Courage	Entertain
Openness	Balance	Wealth
Religion	Compassion	Speed
Order	Fitness	Power
Advancement	Professionalism	Affection
Finances	Relationship	Cooperation
Gratitude	Knowledge	Encouragement
Grace	Patience	Pride in Your Work
Endurance	Change	Clarity
Facilitation	Prosperity	Fun-Loving
Effectiveness	Wellness	Charisma
Fun	Enjoyment	Humour
Fame	Entrepreneurship	Leadership
Justice	Happiness	Renewal
Appreciation	Harmony	Home
Willingness	Peace	Authenticity
Trusting Your Gut	Self-Respect	Contentment
Patience	Abundance	Giving People a Chance
Forgiveness	Reciprocity	

Consider how your values differ from those in your workplace, your community, or in other cultures.

My secret weapons...
(character, values, beliefs)

Life doesn't come with a manual. You build it as you go, sometimes we get things wrong, or we are thrown off course. The key is to ensure you have the skills necessary to get back on track and continue your journey.

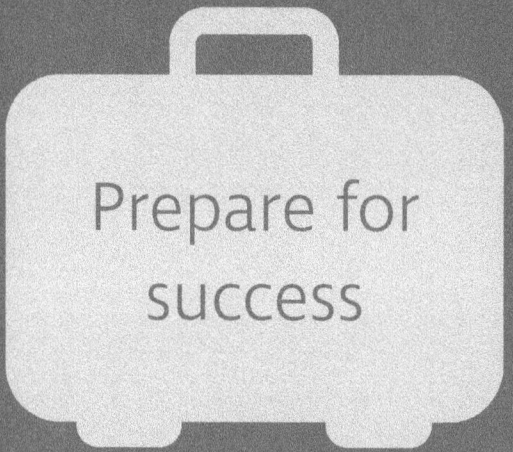

Prepare for success

Habits to rituals

Waking up and getting out of bed, going for a morning run, brushing your teeth, grabbing a coffee, turning on the TV @ 7 pm each night and so on. These are all forms of habits that a cue has triggered (see habit cycle below). Our habits are in everything we do.

The secret is to ensure our good habits become routine or turn into rituals. They need to be consciously actioned (see response below followed by a reward).

A ritual is another level again; it is when a habit doesn't feel like a chore. It is generally something you are passionate about that gives you purpose and meaning. Like the examples, you have captured in 'finding flow'.

The habit cycle:

1. a cue
   (wake up)

2. a craving
   (a coffee)

3. a response
   (head to cafe/kitchen, order/make coffee)

4. a reward
   (the aroma from the coffee, the first sip, energised, awake)

My habits

Some of our habits are good; these are the **positive** habits that will help us flourish; others can be harmful or **negative** habits that require attention or removal from temptation.

Make a list of your daily and weekly habits, the time they occur and mark down if they are positive (+) or negative (–) or not sure (n).

Example – I exercise each morning for 30 minutes (+), I eat chocolate at 3 pm every day (–)

My habits

More daily habits

You can often change your circumstances by changing your attitude.

Eleanor Roosevelt, civil rights activist and former US first lady

Designing a new path

Using the habit cycle, you can identify what triggers your habits and then change your practices or create new positive habits.

To limit your negative or bad habits, you need to find a way to remove the temptation. You've heard the saying, 'out of sight out of mind'; this helps limit temptation. E.g., removing the lolly jar off the counter.

A simple way to introduce a new habit is to build onto an existing good practice. For instance, you are introducing flossing your teeth. You can place your floss beside your toothbrush and remind yourself that you will now floss after cleaning your teeth. Or put a sign or picture on your bathroom mirror as a reminder.

In the incredible book **Atomic Habits by James Clear**, he recommends using the two-minute rule when introducing a new habit. Try to start with something that you can achieve within two minutes. E.g., two minutes of meditation or a 2 minute walk each day. Find an activity you will enjoy and do this for a week and then build on it slowly; before you know it, you will be doing an hour a day and finding your flow. **It would help if you liked it to commit to it.**

These small positive changes will start to become routine and will establish new habit patterns. This same method applies to your focus areas in your compass and any other goals you set. The key is finding habits that you enjoy, not those trending, if you prefer walking over cycling than walk.

Look at it as making positive change one degree at a time. What small change will you create today?

My new path

Capture some positive habits built around your existing good practices and introduce a habit that can be achieved within 2 minutes. Don't forget the most powerful motivator of all is YOU. It's your determination that ultimately sets you on your new path; you can do it.

Tracking my habits

Track your habit progress. Use the calendar below to record what, when and where for your new habit. Place a tick on the days you complete it. Try not to miss a day; doing something is better than nothing.

E.g., my new habit is to walk for 10 mins around the block @ 5 pm each day with my dog. Or every Tuesday @ 10 am, I will meditate for 2 minutes

Day 1	Day 2	Day 3	Day 4	Day 5	Day 6
Day 7	Day 8	Day 9	Day 10	Day 11	Day 12
Day 13	Day 14	Day 15	Day 16	Day 17	Day 18
Day 19	Day 20	Day 21	Day 22	Day 23	Day 24
Day 25	Day 26	Day 27	Day 28	Day 29	Day 30

Tracking my habits

Track another habit here.
My new behaviour is:

Day 1	Day 2	Day 3	Day 4	Day 5	Day 6
Day 7	Day 8	Day 9	Day 10	Day 11	Day 12
Day 13	Day 14	Day 15	Day 16	Day 17	Day 18
Day 19	Day 20	Day 21	Day 22	Day 23	Day 24
Day 25	Day 26	Day 27	Day 28	Day 29	Day 30

Looking back over the month – include a smiley face or something of your choosing to represent if this habit has now become a routine or a ritual.

We are what we repeatedly do. Excellence, then, is not an act but a habit.

Aristotle, Greek philosopher

Adapt and flourish

A positive attitude is what you need to succeed. When you learn to adapt, you will be ready for anything.

If you do not know how to do something, **learn to do it**.
When you run into a problem, **work through it**.
Need another skill, **master it**.

Throughout our lives, we will often be faced with a decision to either adapt and move forward or remain unchanged and get left behind.

Your ancestors may have some brilliant examples of how they adapted to survive as mine had. Or you can look to nature for some incredible examples of adaption; for instance, the Forest red gum Eucalyptus tereticornis and Jacaranda trees are highly adaptable to their environment.

Be brave and choose to adapt every time.

Be more like a turtle

Turtles, like octopuses, are also highly adaptive to their environment – some turtle species can start life as carnivores and, depending on their territory, evolve to herbivores or omnivores. Their shells and feet also adapt to the environment.

Based on certain conditions, including temperature changes, baby turtles can influence their gender by moving around inside their eggs. This is a condition known as temperature-dependent sex determination or TSD. Very clever.

They are one of the oldest reptile groups globally – older than snakes, crocodiles and alligators and date back over 200 million years.

Turtles have learned a thing or two about adaption. Be like a turtle!

As the turtle is also my spirit animal, I have a clear bias toward them.

Have you discovered what your spirit animal might be? There are some great quizzes online (search **spirit animal quiz** and find out what yours is).

Sometimes the road you are on leads nowhere, so choose another path.

My unique connections

Discover more about spirit animals, a pet, favourite plant, or something else that you connect with, other than people. Write something interesting about it here.

My people connections

Capture the positive connections you have in your life. Those connections are reliable through good and bad times and give you the reassurance and positive support you need.

Why are they so important to you, and what do you think you mean to them?

There is nothing either good or bad, but thinking makes it so.

William Shakespeare, English playwright

We are what we think

Your past experiences, beliefs, fears, biases, and environment are all reference points that will influence your decisions, how you feel about something, and how you will achieve your goals.

There is a lot of literature today about how our experiences can alter our brain's function, showing it is a more adaptable organ than you might think.

Being open to ideas, viewing challenges as opportunities, being inspired by the success of others, persisting despite obstacles, and being able to learn from constructive feedback will allow your brain to get the exercise it needs for optimal health. This is a growth mindset.

However, having a fixed mindset is the opposite; it is generally closed to ideas, focused on avoidance, critical of change and full of doubt.

Ultimately, we are each responsible for how we think.

Which mindset do you think you have?

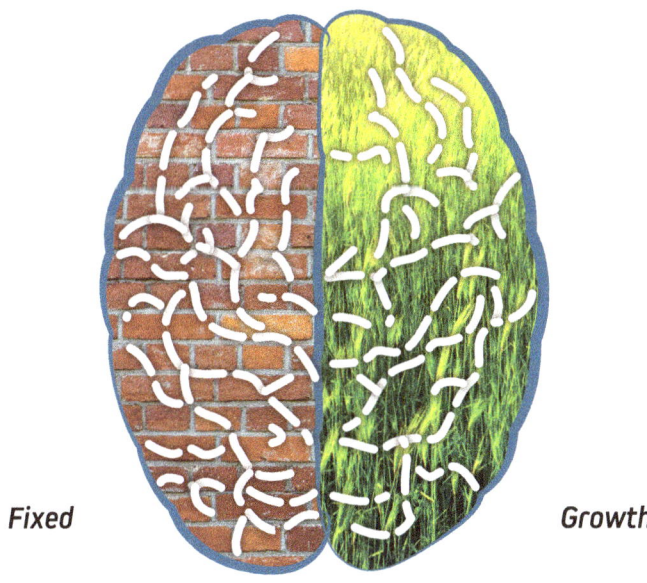

Fixed　　　　　　　　　　　　Growth

My mindset

I have a _____ mindset.
Why do you believe this?

Move towards growth

Every time you catch yourself with a 'fixed mindset, you can either put $1 into a 'swear jar'(expensive) or acknowledge that you are doing this by writing it down or talking it through. To truly let something go, you need to feel it fully.

For example: What am I thinking right now? What evidence do I have for this thought? Is this thought true? Will it happen? What advice would you give a good friend thinking the same way?

The other option is to reframe the thought and turn it into a growth option. For example: from 'I look terrible in this outfit' to 'This outfit makes me look smart' or 'I can't' to 'I cant at the moment, I can if I have more time'.

Remember, your brain is like a muscle; it gets stronger when you use it and repeat positive actions.

Reframing my fixed mindsets

Write down some of the strong emotional thoughts you have had or fixed mindsets you have had to reframe.

Start each day with an act of kindness, end with gratitude.

Expressing gratitude

Do not wait to express your gratitude; the time may never come. Seize every opportunity. Write down or tell someone what you are grateful for today.

I am grateful for...

Saying thanks and expressing gratitude is just what you do.

I have arrived; I am home, in the here and the now. I am solid; I am free in the ultimate I dwell.

Buddhist monk, Thich Nhat Hanh

Savouring the moment

Practice the act of savouring often and describe how it feels. I used to sit by the beach every morning watching the waves roll in before I faced my day, and it was incredible.

Here's an exercise to try. Look at the picture on this page or one of your own. Take in every detail of what you see, hear, feel, taste, and smell around you. Concentrate on the water you are drifting through, feel the warmth of the sun on your face, smell the fresh air as it fills your lungs. Be in the moment ...

Bliss, savour it.

Savour some more

Keep practising the act of savouring and describe how it feels. What did you savour today?

If you work with people, plants or animals, and being kind is difficult for you, ask for a transfer to

Mars

Kindness brings peace

Practice kindness always.
Even when someone doesn't take the first step to smile or say hello, that doesn't mean you need to wait. Be first, lead the way to kindness.

It is not hard to offer something as simple as a smile when you walk past a stranger or to give words of comfort to someone in need.

Kindness does not expect anything in return; it is the joy of giving to others and yourself. Kindness provides something more valuable than material things – it is a giving of yourself and your presence.

How often do you practice kindness, how does it make you feel?

Carry out a random act of kindness, with no expectation of reward, safe in the knowledge that one day someone might do the same for you.

Diana, Princess of Wales

I am strong

Creating your affirmations – **a statement or action for emotional support or encouragement** – is inspiring. They are great mindful habits that work well in helping you to achieve your goals. Capture your affirmations below. Include the promise, why it is essential, what activities you will do and when you will do them. E.g., 'I choose to be hopeful so that I can reconnect with my life and my family. I will practice mindfulness daily, starting today for 1 minute and build up until I reach 10 minutes each day.

My affirmations

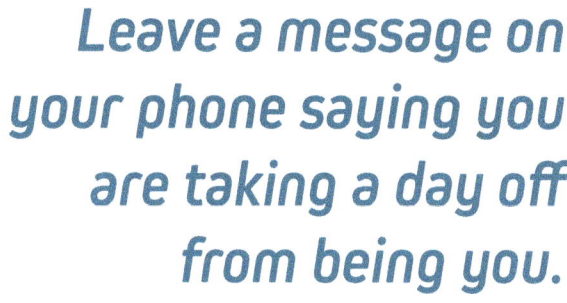

Leave a message on your phone saying you are taking a day off from being you.

Visualise your success

As with your affirmations, forming a mental picture of something is also an excellent mindful habit to help you achieve success. I practised this when I needed to present to a large group, and I would practise visualising what the group would look like, how the room was set up, how I was projecting to the room and how good it felt once I had delivered the message.

This is a great exercise when trying to overcome your fears; practice visualising a positive outcome. Write down some visualising activities you want to try.

We have each been given this gift of life including the incredible planet surrounding us. Let's try to tread lightly, minimize or reuse where possible and leave this place in good order for the next generation.

Simplify your life

Reduce or remove all unnecessary 'stuff' in your life; focus on those areas that give you a sense of purpose, achievement, or connection.

Make a list of what you can remove today?

Less is more
What else can go?

All seasons

Do not wait until the spring to have a cleanout. Donate or recycle anything you did not use at the end of each season. Write a list of what will go each season.

A mantra from William Morris: 'If you want a golden rule that will fit everybody, this is it: Have nothing in your houses that you do not know to be useful or believe to be beautiful.'

From: 'The Beauty of Life', a lecture before the Birmingham Society of Arts and School of Design (19 February 1880)

SPRING	SUMMER	AUTUMN	WINTER

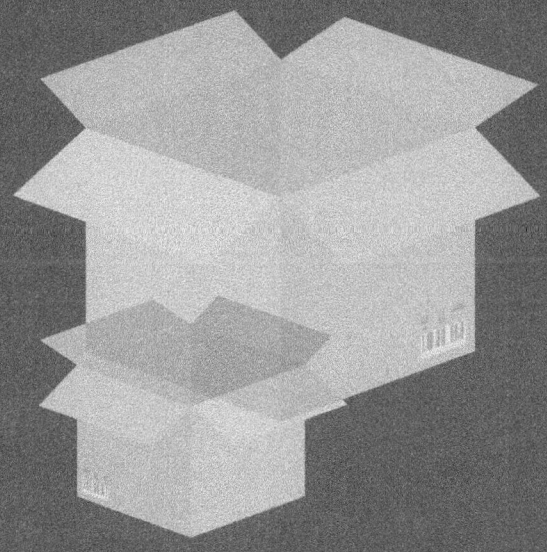

As we let our light shine, we unconsciously give other people permission to do the same.

Nelson Mandela, anti-apartheid campaigner and former South African president

Every new sunrise is an opportunity to reset your intention for the day.

Checking in as you go, is essential. You don't want to discover you have wandered too far off course before making corrections.

Am I on track?

Status update 1

Each week get into the practice of checking in with your progress. Are you moving towards your goals? Do you need to adjust your objectives to continue? Start with a goal that can be achieved in 4-5 weeks and then build on them.

Remember to ask yourself:
- What went well this week?
- Did anything stop me from achieving/setting my objectives?
- If so, what might be the underlying fear or cause?
- Does this fear impact my life in other ways?

Status update 2

Are you still on track? Keep tracking your progress.

keep going

You must do the thing you think you cannot do.

Eleanor Roosevelt, civil rights activist and former US first lady

Many of the truths that we hold onto depend on social prejudices.

Status update 3

Keep going. Nobody said it was going to be easy.

You've got this

Happiness Check-in

Measuring your happiness can be difficult, so I ask a different question, how content are you right now? Thinking about this moment, do you feel like everything is ok, or do you desire something else, or more. Using the guide below, which face best describes how content you are with life now? Record the number, time, and date. Check-in as often as you like. Note if it changes each time.

1   2   3   4

Right now I'm feeling like a ( ) __/__/__ @ __:__

Right now I'm feeling like a ( ) __/__/__ @ __:__

Right now I'm feeling like a ( ) __/__/__ @ __:__

Right now I'm feeling like a ( ) __/__/__ @ __:__

Right now I'm feeling like a ( ) __/__/__ @ __:__

Right now I'm feeling like a ( ) __/__/__ @ __:__

Right now I'm feeling like a ( ) __/__/__ @ __:__

Right now I'm feeling like a ( ) __/__/__ @ __:__

Status update 4

Almost there, you've got this; keep going.

almost there

If you spend you life comparing yourself to others, what will be your legacy?

Status update 5

You are on the home stretch

What insights do you have to share with others as they embark on their journey? What are some of the highlights for you?

home stretch

Nothing ever goes away until it teaches us what we need to know.

Pema Chödrön, American Buddhist teacher, author, nun and mother

You will make mistakes,
99% guaranteed.

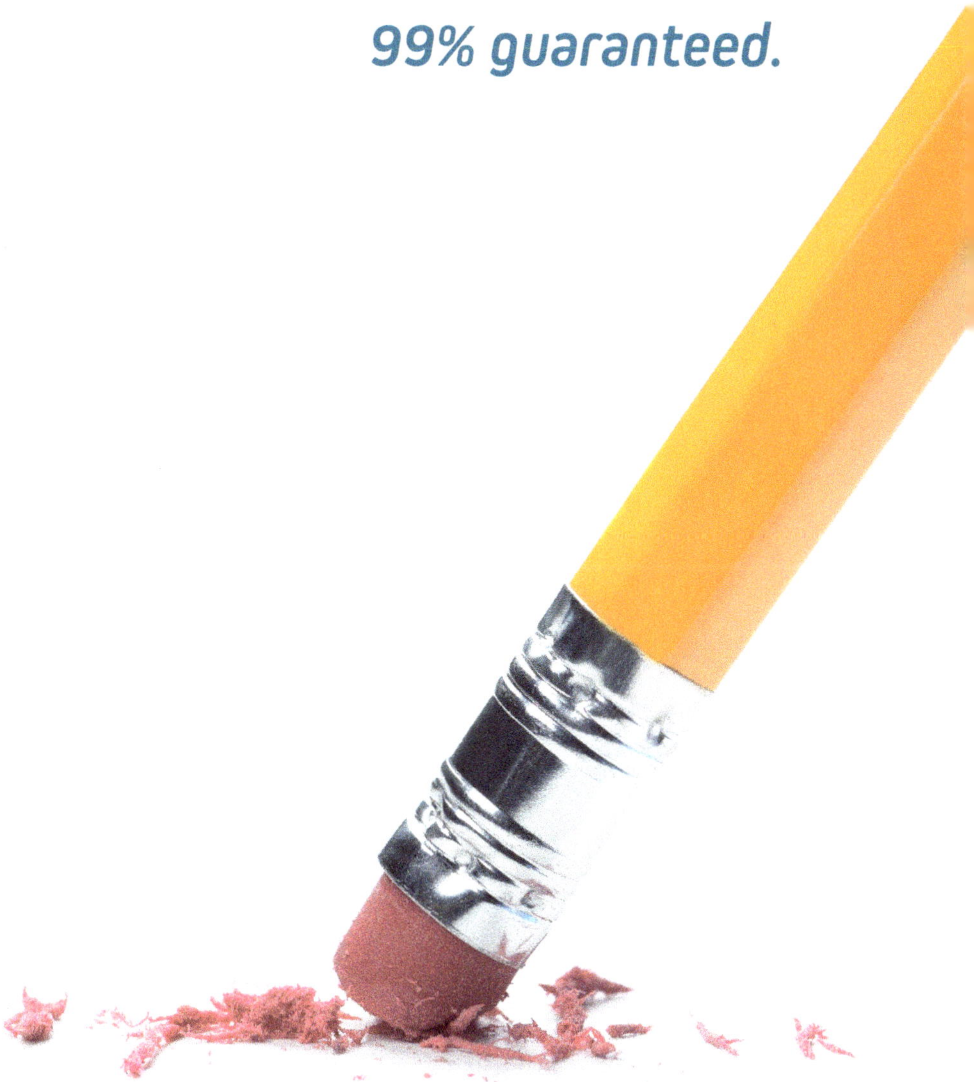

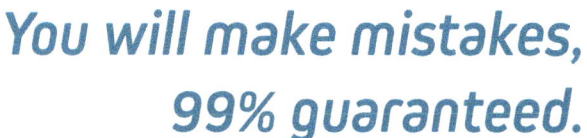

How my happiness changes

Track how your happiness changes throughout the day. Is it different from morning to night? Is there a 'happy day' of the week? Refer to your happiness check-in for clues.

Life, it's a balancing act

To find that 'sweet spot' in life, where you are flourishing, requires regular checking of your compass. Is it still pointing in the right direction, or have you wandered off course?

Below is another way to check-in and keep things balanced in life. I use it in conjunction with my life compass. This simple tally system includes a ranking out of five to see if my assets outweigh my liabilities. You can change the focus points and have whatever works for you.

Life Assets		Life Liabilities	
Good Health	IIII	Poor Health	I
Knowledge	III	Lack of Knowledge	I
Skills	III	Lack of Skills	
Positive Habits	III	Poor Habits	II
Positive Character trait	III	Poor Character trait	II
Positive Emotion	IIII	Negative Emotion	II
Purpose	II	Lack of Purpose	
Positive Relationships	IIII	Poor Relationships	I

Try this for yourself using the Life Balance template on the next page as your guide.

My Life Balance sheet
How do I stack up?

Life Assets	Life Liabilities
Good Health	Poor Health
Knowledge	Lack of Knowledge
Skills	Lack of Skills
Positive Habits	Poor Habits
Positive Character trait	Poor Character trait
Positive Emotion	Negative Emotion
Purpose	Lack of Purpose
Positive Relationships	Poor Relationships

So, how is it going?

Write down how you feel now. Do you feel any different from when you started using your compass? If so, how? What advice would you give to anyone using these tools?

Yes, there are scary bits on the journey, but they become great stories to share with others.

Change is just a fact of life. When things happen, we need to find a way forward. It can be scary, but with support it is doable.

Disruption, Change direction

**Change will not come if we wait for some other person or some other time.
We are the ones we've been waiting for. We are the change that we seek.**

Barack Obama, former US President

You are the only one who can conquer your fears, and when you do, you will become invincible.

Facing your fears

Do you have fears that are holding you back from achieving your goals?

Practice the art of 'facing your fears, as avoiding them only intensifies them.

Consider what you are afraid of; practice using the steps below and saying to yourself, 'it's you or me, I choose me'. Repeat this often.

Over time this practice shows how you can quickly disarm your fears when you are prepared to face them. It is uncomfortable at first but rewarding when you practice it often.

I got my partner to try this approach before he flew anywhere. He was a terrible flyer, and nowadays, he can now make it through a whole flight without a sick bag.

Try these steps and start slowly:

1. Write down what it is that is stopping you from achieving your goals. (**Too much competition, I am not good enough, people say I cannot do this, I'm scared of failure, I'm afraid of flying, it's too late to change**)
2. Evaluate your fears, on a scale of 1–10, of how scary they genuinely are.
3. Rethink your thinking – sometimes we see our goals as obligations (**I must fly to X today, lose 5kg, and finish this project**).
4. Reframe your thinking to be an opportunity. (**When I fly to X today, I will get to do Y, losing 5kg means I can fit into that dress, how good will I feel when I finish this project and start something new**).
5. Reflect on a time when you did conquer your fears. How did it make you feel?
6. Seek professional support if your fears are debilitating, and you cannot face them on your own.

My fears

What fears, if any, are stopping you from moving forward with your goals in life? How could you reframe your thoughts towards these fears?

Change your focus

Have you ever had a time when you were overthinking something, like whether you made the right impression, not getting your message across in a meeting, if you completed a task correctly, or maybe you have been concentrating for too long and need a break?

It is time to change the focus.

I used to do a 3 pm chair yoga session in my workplace. About that time, you were either looking for the vending machine for a snack or needed a walk around the block to recharge.

My top ten state changers and great ideas to mix things up:

1. Get up and stretch – yep, just stretch and take a few breaths
2. Exercise – take a walk around the park, or go for a ride
3. Phone a friend, or say hello to your neighbour
4. Eat or cook something that makes you feel good
5. Colour in, do a puzzle, draw, or write something
6. Listen to music, dance
7. Do some gardening
8. Meditate or yoga
9. Read a book
10. Use a mirror or record a message to check your tone, how are you projecting, e.g., how you might be coming across to others, is your voice loud, muffled.

Intelligence is the ability to adapt to change.

Stephen Hawking, British physicist and cosmologist

It's okay not to be okay. Not every day includes sunshine; you can rest assured that it will shine again.

Be wild, do something different

Sometimes you just need a change of scenery. Try taking a new route to work, a new hairdo, order something different from the menu, turn the television off, invent your own board game, dance in the dark, or cook something you've never tried before.

When was the last time you did something for the first time?

Me being different

What did I do differently? How did it feel?

Every truth has two sides; it is as well to look at both before we commit ourselves to either.

Aesop, Greek storyteller

Unless you have evidence of the truth, do not buy into rumour or media bias. There are plenty of innocent people suffering because of herd mentality.

Perception vs reality

Change your perception, change your reality. Perception is your perspective based upon your experiences, and your reality comprises a series of experiences that shape how you see things.

What do you see below? What do others see? Try to imagine there is another view that is not your own, and that is okay. I'll tell you what some people see on the next page

What do you see?

Perception vs reality

Have you ever jumped to a conclusion only to discover you were wrong? How did it feel? Did you apologise? How could this be avoided in the future?

PICTURE: A tree and two faces.

If you don't like something, change it. If you can't change it, change your attitude.

Maya Angelou, American poet and activist

Rethinking your values

Remember, our values are what we decide they will be. Looking at your values today (or what you have captured earlier in the book), are your values holding you back or helping you forward? Why?

Consciously choosing your values can alter your destiny.

My revised values

Consciously choosing your values can change your destiny.

What do your values need to be to enable you to reach your full potential?

> *I need to remain true and authentic in all that I do.*

Beliefs

Beliefs drive us; values guide us.

A belief is an idea that a person holds to be true, irrespective of whether it is the truth or not.

Beliefs can either prevent or help us achieve our life goals, like having a fixed or growth mindset.

Beliefs can change. Like values, you get to decide what you want to believe in.

How do your beliefs stack up? Are they still true for you?

Beliefs

What are some of the good things you believe about yourself?

If you are going to model something, make accountability a non-negotiable element.

Sorry, my mistake

Sometimes we think it is easier to play the 'blame game'; however, it doesn't work in the long run. Unfortunately, you end up repeating this behaviour and struggle ever to be accountable for your actions. We all make mistakes in life; our failures are what help us to learn and grow. If we don't accept our own mistakes, how do we evolve and become better humans?

I've done this myself, and it does hold you back. Once I realised how it made me feel, I chose a different path.

Have you ever blamed someone else for something you did? How did it feel? What message would you give to someone that blames others?

Taking responsibility

Going from victim to victor is a choice. By taking responsibility for your life and actions, you get to be in the driver's seat. You stop being a passenger and passively observing as life goes by, complaining or blaming others when things go wrong.

Life doesn't always give us what we want; however, we choose how to respond to life's challenges. When you take the position of responsibility, you become empowered, and this is how you get to take back control of your life.

The energy we project, our feelings, thoughts and actions are the energy we receive. If we project positive energy, the response will be to feel good.

So, would you agree, it pays to take responsibility for your life?

You've come this far, don't stop now. Find the momentum you need to push forward if you are stuck or need motivation.

There is no such thing as can't.

Albert Hall (my dad, my hero)

Getting unstuck

Sometimes we just get stuck and need a bit of a nudge to keep going again. Using a reference point from when you've been stuck before can help.

Write down a time when you were stuck. When was it, where were you, who were you with, how did it feel? How did you get unstuck?

When I was stuck

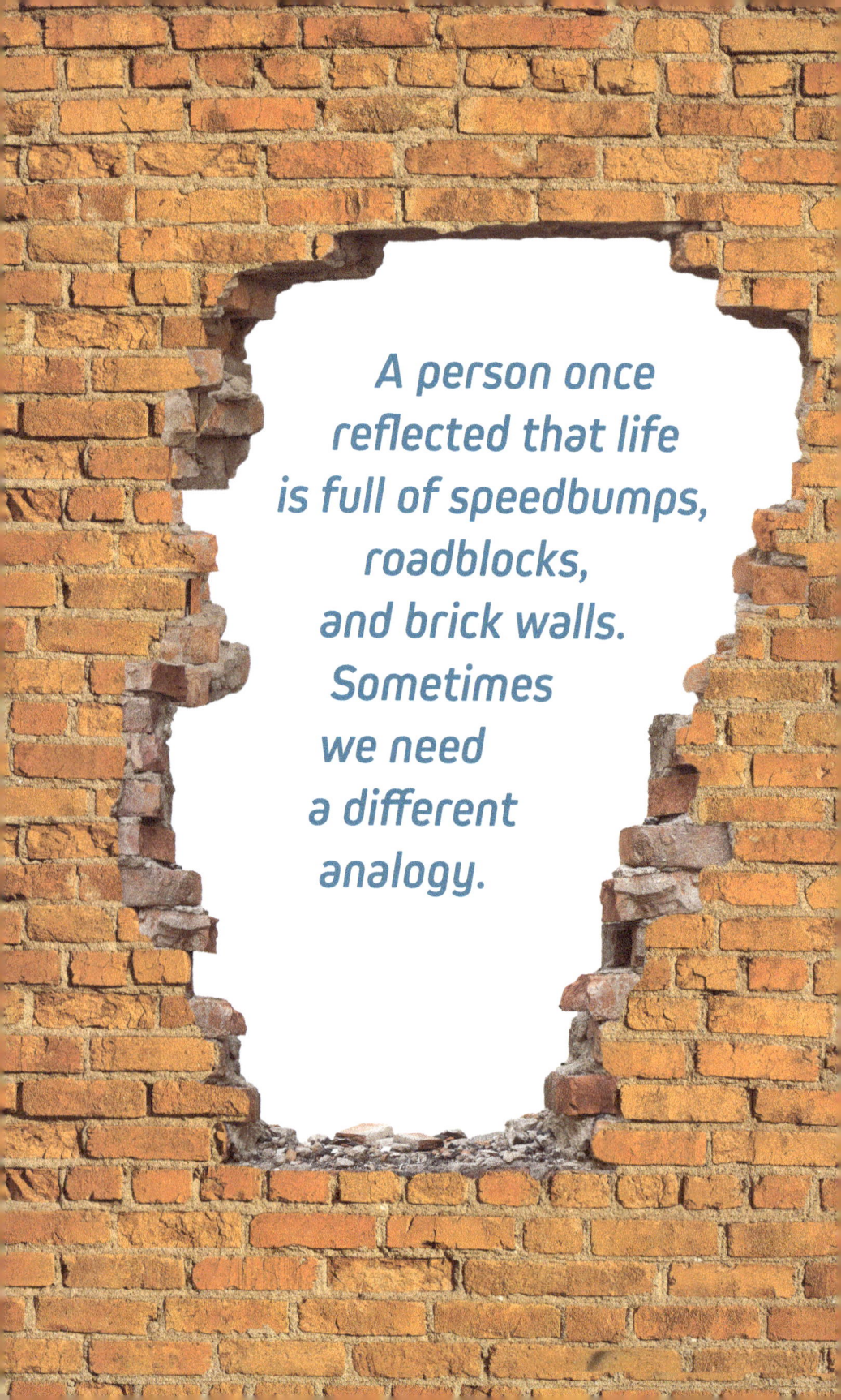

A person once reflected that life is full of speedbumps, roadblocks, and brick walls. Sometimes we need a different analogy.

What a great idea

Did you know that taking some time to capture your ideas and thoughts can help you to get unstuck? I recommend finding some quiet space to capture any new ideas or thoughts that come to mind. Look back at what you captured earlier, again they don't have to make sense now.

Something I found helpful in doing this exercise is to use a mind map. You can do a search on mind maps for more information on how it. An example might be buying a car. I would write that at the centre of the page and then write the first five things that come to mind when thinking about buying a car (E.g., finance, model, mileage, size, colour). From here, I would do another five things for each of these headings and repeat this once more.

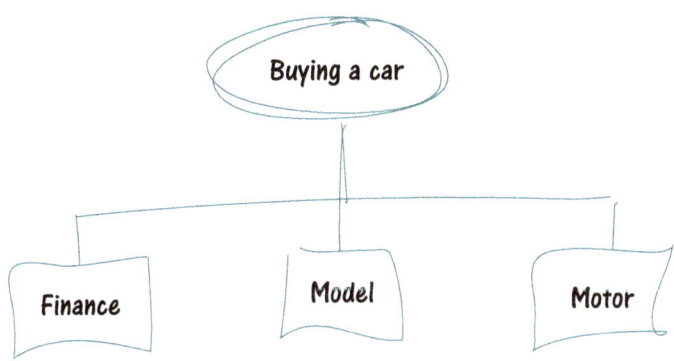

You'll be surprised how much information is captured from this simple exercise.

More brilliant ideas

Hop onto the change rollercoaster and hold on for the ride.

What we do now echoes in eternity.

Marcus Aurelius,
Roman emperor and Stoic philosopher

Getting motivated

I have captured a few of my favourite books and songs. These are some of the sources that inspire or motive me.

Stillness speaks – Eckhart Tolle
The Rosie Project – Graeme Simsion
Who moved my cheese – Spencer Johnson
Let's pretend this never happened – Jenny Lawson
The boy, the mole, the fox, and the horse – Charlie Mackesy
The seven spiritual laws of success – Deepak Chopra
The little book of behaviour investing – James Montier
Time – Alexander Waugh
The alchemist – Paul Coelho
Atomic habits – James Clear
It's ok that you're not ok – Megan Devine
Predictably irrational – Dr Dan Ariely
Sapiens – Yuval Noah Harari
Why smart people hurt – Eric Maisel
The diary of a young girl – Anne Frank
The power of moments – Chip & Dan Heath

Maria's top picks

Rise up – Andra Day
Bonfire Heart – James Blunt
Wiyathul – Geoffrey Gurrumul Yunupingu
Ain't no mountain high enough – Marvin Gaye
Head above water – Avril Lavigne
I am, I said – Neil Diamond
Fix you – Coldplay
Brave – Sara Bareilles
Lose yourself – Eminem
True colours – Cyndi Lauper
Don't stop believing – Journey
Stronger (What doesn't kill you) – Kelly Clarkson
Walking on sunshine – Katrina and the waves
Whatever it takes – Imagine Dragons
What am I to you? – Norah Jones

Maria's playlist

My motivators

Capture your list of books, songs, poetry, movies etc., that inspire you. Others could include affirmations you have created to motivate yourself, your work, hobbies, friends, coach, mentor, whatever.

Sometimes the only thing that will make a difference is chocolate, a cup of tea, and a Disney movie.

Celebrate along the way

It can be daunting to try and look too far ahead. Remember that we get one chance, so **TAKE THE TIME TO ENJOY THE JOURNEY** – the destination is already known.

Do the '20 things that make me happy. Use the following pages to capture your celebrating life.

Celebrating life

I need to remember...

Use these pages to write down anything else important to you as you navigate your way through life's journey. If I hear of a good book, saying or piece of advice, I jot it down to refer to it later.

Notes

Notes

My life is my message.

Mahatma Gandhi,
Indian proponent of non-violence

Final thoughts

LIFE is an incredible gift, despite the many hurdles we might face at times. You get to decide your legacy, but do not wait until it is too late.

Extend yourself, go beyond yesterday, eat what you know is good for your body, exercise your body and thoughts daily.

Start with the end in mind and work your way backwards, setting goals along the way. Sure, obstacles will get in the way of your plans at times, and nobody said it would be easy.

Easy is boring. Where is the challenge in that? Be newsworthy, daring, take risks, turn left if everyone else turns right, see what is behind that corner.

Nobody discovered anything by sitting at home in front of the television pondering. Go out into the world, and learn how you fit into it.

Don't blame others when things become difficult or you can't see your way out. This is when you will need to be courageous and find a way to accept your circumstances to rebuild and move on.

Learn from your successes and failures. You will need to experience both to appreciate what life is all about genuinely. Create your own story and remain curious.

Be brave, kind, and authentic always.

Maria

www.ingramcontent.com/pod-product-compliance
Lightning Source LLC
Chambersburg PA
CBHW040240010526
44107CB00065B/2819